ARIZONA ACROSS 400 YEARS
Episodes from a Colorful Past

ARIZONA ACROSS 400 YEARS
Episodes from a Colorful Past

JOHN PHILIP WILSON

SUNSTONE
PRESS

SANTA FE

Sunstone books may be purchased for educational, business, or sales promotional use.
For information please write: Special Markets Department, Sunstone Press,
P.O. Box 2321, Santa Fe, New Mexico 87504-2321.

Book and cover design › R. Ahl
Printed on acid-free paper
∞
eBook 978-1-61139-629-4
*

Library of Congress Cataloging-in-Publication Data

Names: Wilson, John P. (John Philip), 1935- author.
Title: Arizona across 400 years : episodes from a colorful past / by John
    Philip Wilson.
Other titles: Arizona across four hundred years
Description: Santa Fe, NM : Sunstone Press, [2021] | Includes
    bibliographical references | Summary: "A collection of episodes, from
    the earliest European explorations of Arizona in the 1500s to the early
    twentieth century, that includes both little-known and more familiar
    events"-- Provided by publisher
Identifiers: LCCN 2021021149 | ISBN 9781632933355 (paperback) | ISBN
    9781611396294 (epub)
Subjects:
Classification: LCC F811.6 .W55 2021 | DDC 979.1--dc23
LC record available at https://lccn.loc.gov/2021021149

WWW.SUNSTONEPRESS.COM
SUNSTONE PRESS / POST OFFICE BOX 2321 / SANTA FE, NM 87504-2321 /USA
(505) 988-4418 / FAX (505) 988-1025

To Harwood Hinton, longtime professor of history, editor, and valued friend.

Preface ◊ 8

1. Where Did Coronado Cross Arizona? ◊ 11

2. The First Corrals in the Southwest ◊ 22

3. Awatovi—New Light on a Legend ◊ 30

4. Fort Yuma: Hottest Post in All Creation? ◊ 36

5. Tucson As It Was in 1858–1861 ◊ 38

6. Early Days of Newspapering in the Southwest ◊ 41

7. Jefferson Davis' Railroad Dream
      Becomes a Mail Line to California ◊ 45

8. Scouting in the Chiricahuas: July 1864 ◊ 53

9. Stage Robbing—In the Buff? ◊ 66

10. Encounter at Picacho Pass ◊ 68

11. Two Young Heroes of Early Arizona ◊ 72

12. Farming for Feathers! ◊ 75

13. The House by the Side of the Road ◊ 82

14. Black Gold in the San Simon ◊ 93

Suggested Readings ◊ 106

PREFACE

In these pages, we'll recount fourteen episodes from Arizona's storied past; articles that shed new light on unfamiliar corners of our state. One perennial topic has been the route of Spanish explorer Francisco Vásquez de Coronado, or simply Coronado, as he trekked across southeastern Arizona in search of the fabled Seven Cities of Cibola. These were the pueblos of the Zuni Indians in far western New Mexico. Many writers have sought to document the course of his journey in 1540–1542, but a resolution is unlikely to come anytime soon, for good reasons.

Later in the sixteenth century, other Spaniards laid the foundation for a horse corral that may be the oldest European construction in the southwestern United States, perhaps in North America. A century later, the native pueblo of Awatovi was destroyed by Hopi Indians of the same tribe, an event noted in the service record of a Spanish soldier who saw the ruins of the site several months afterwards.

Present-day Arizona became part of the missionary province of Sonora at the end of the 1600s, but it experienced only limited attempts at Spanish settlement until well into the next century. Northern Arizona was joined to the United States in 1848, after the Mexican War, while the southern tier of the territory was added only in 1856. By this time, would-be silver miners from the eastern U.S. had been drawn into the Tubac-Tucson region, administered as an extension of New Mexico Territory. The native population there was primarily Papago and Pima Indians, with an admixture of Mexican settlers from the south. The mountainous regions were the domain of the Apache Indians.

Tucson in the 1850s and for some years later had an unattractive appearance in the eyes of visitors, but it was home to a newspaper as early as 1859 and became a focal point of then-Senator Jefferson Davis' vision of a southern transcontinental railroad. His dream achieved reality briefly when Confederate mail riders reached all the way to southern California in the late spring and summer of 1861.

A Union army of California volunteers chased out the company of Confederates that occupied Tucson in 1862, and inherited the problem of how to deal with the hostile Apaches, who seemed to be everywhere outside of the few settled areas. The soldiers operated from adobe forts which they built themselves; these never became pleasant places to live. Raiding continued into the middle 1880s while outlaws occasioned many anxious moments for travelers.

Although Arizona's economic prospects were originally tied to mining, the Phoenix area and then the middle and upper Gila River valley experienced a surge in irrigated agriculture after the Civil War. Along the upper Little Colorado River, one farmer tried to homestead on land that wasn't open for claiming, with unhappy results. In the major river valleys, a new industry bloomed after 1892 until the beginning of World War I—raising ostriches for the plumes used in fashionable ladies' hats, boas, and fans. At the time, no one thought of eating one!

Topics such as these I explored in writing for *Arizona Senior World*, a monthly newspaper issued in Gilbert, Arizona. Other potential stories came to light from examining an endless series of late-nineteenth newspapers on microfilm, and by reading National Archives microfilms with reports of Army scouts. The Coronado article reflects a long-standing interest and first drew my own attention during an archaeological project at Fort Huachuca.

One of my earlier books, *Islands in the Desert,* was originally a contract history written for Coronado National Forest, and another contract led to the recording of several old oil-well-drilling locations as historical archaeological sites. The discoveries of oil in neighboring states had prompted local businessmen to drill in Arizona, in hopes of finding reserves. Success eluded them except in the far northeastern corner of the state.

The decision to make a book of such accounts followed a suggestion by Dr. Harwood Hinton, a good friend and highly-respected professor of history at the University of Arizona. He had seen some of my writings scattered through publications unfamiliar to historians, and thought they deserved a wider audience. These have no necessary connections from one to another and were written originally over almost forty years. Half have not been published previously; the others I rewrote to varying degrees. Acknowledgements are owing to Dr. Hinton and to Gilbert H. Moore of Tucson, the latter a retired editor at *Arizona Senior World*; to the Arizona Geological Survey and Arizona

Corporation Commission; and to Drs. Pat Gilman and Pat Spoerl, for whom I produced several contract reports. I also appreciate the opportunities extended by J. Thomas Via and Duane Bock of Tucson Electric Power Company, which enabled me to expand routine clearance surveys into mini-research projects.

Readers should feel free to select whatever interests them; the articles are variable in their subjects as well as their lengths. Hopefully they may provide a measure of entertainment as well as an inspiration to learn more about Arizona's rich history. Original research is always a challenge, but it may lead to generous rewards.

I

Where Did Coronado Cross Arizona?

His friends and followers called him Francisco Vásquez, but we know him as Coronado. One hundred and fifty years before Father Eusebio Kino set foot in southern Arizona, Francisco Vásquez de Coronado led a small army of Spanish adventurers north from Mexico to look for the fabled Seven Cities of Cibola, rumored to be rich in gold and other treasures. The Viceroy of New Spain appointed him to lead this expedition, naming him as "captain general of certain people for the conquest and settlement of the land discovered by fray Marcos de Niza." Fray Marcos was a Franciscan friar whom the Viceroy had sent in 1539 to discover new lands to the north of Mexico. Now in 1540, those who set out with Coronado expected to discover great wealth, only to see their dreams turn to disappointment two years later.

The 358 or so Spaniards, accompanied by more than 1500 servants and Mexican Indians, headed north from the last Spanish settlement at Culiacán in western Mexico. They rode through what are now the Mexican states of Sinaloa and Sonora, then across some 150 miles of present-day southeastern Arizona. Historical researchers have long sought to pinpoint their actual route, and in recent years a petroleum geologist, a prominent Arizona political figure, and a suspense novelist, among others, have all attempted to retrace the earlier trek.

This might have been easier if "a painting from this [portion of the] journey" had survived. Coronado ordered this made after the expedition arrived in Cibola, the country of the Zuni Indians, and sent it back to the Viceroy. Because he had sent the painting, Francisco Vásquez refrained from describing the route of his journey in words. Later in the same letter he said that "I am sending paintings of all this to Your Lordship [the Viceroy], along with the route." Neither this hide (or hides?), which probably amounted to less than a map, nor any other contemporary depiction of the route is known to exist today.

People who have sought to trail the explorer through Arizona have found that without maps, this isn't easy. Because of his failure to discover new riches, Coronado's expedition was soon forgotten except by a few historians in Mexico. The documents that have survived are an assorted lot, some of them contemporary and others written twenty years or so after this epic journey. Historian Herbert Eugene Bolton once made a list of all the internal references to missing documents, maps, and so forth, "to tantalize scholars forever."

After the United States acquired the present American Southwest during the Mexican War, people began to write about Coronado's discoveries. Names, distances and descriptions in the surviving narratives made it relatively easy to identify the Hopi Indian towns and many of the Indian pueblos in New Mexico. While the army made few side trips, one reconnaissance party under Garcia López de Cárdenes clearly visited the south rim of the Grand Canyon. But these sources contain only vague and incomplete references to the expedition's course between its departure point at Culiacán, in the present Mexican state of Sinaloa, and Cibola, the Zuni Indian pueblos some 300 leagues (about 790 miles) distant. No journal or diary of the route exists, nor did the Coronado chroniclers record the names of most of the native peoples whom they met. The extant writings give only a few place names—Corazones, the Valley of Señora, the Rio Nexpa, Valley of Suya and the single most important landmark, Chichilticalli. Chichilticalli, or Chichilticale, means the Red House in the Nahuatl language of Mexico, spoken widely in the sixteenth century.

At this same time, a ship captain who sailed up the lower Colorado River to resupply the expedition (which he never found) identified every native group he met, and some of his terms are still recognizable. The captain, Fernando de Alarcón, also left us a valuable insight from an Indian leader on the lower Colorado, to whom he asserted that The Sun had sent him to tell the people living along the river that they should not make war among themselves. If this was so, the Indian responded "I should tell him the reason why The Sun had not sent me earlier to stifle the wars there had been among them for a very long time which had killed many [people]?" The Indian's point was that the normal state of affairs was for the country to be at war.

The narrative of Pedro de Castañeda among the Coronado documents seems to agree, where he wrote in reference to the Valley of Suya that "It is not known how [chickens] could have penetrated so much *tierra de guerra*, being at war as all [the *pueblos*] are with each other." Again, the same author said that veins of gold had been discovered but the Spaniards at Suya were unable to work these "because the country was at war."

In marked contrast, the Relation del Suceso, a copy of a contemporary record by another member of the expedition, stated that in seventy-three days Coronado reached Cibola from Culiacán, a distance of 300 leagues, and "We found the natives peaceful for the whole way." This would soon change, first at Cibola and then with a war against the Tiwa Indian pueblos along the Rio Grande.

What are we to believe? The writers may not all deserve equal creditability. The most complete narrative is that of Pedro de Casteñada Nájera, who almost certainly had notes at hand and was drafting what he clearly intended to be a book. But he wrote twenty years after everyone had returned to Mexico, and his surviving manuscript is a copy dated 1596. How reliable was he, and what did he not say? This is one example of how the lapse of time, with attendant confusions and seeming contradictions, can creep in to plague translators and historians.

When we turn to place names, none of these except for some Indian pueblos have survived beyond the expedition's own documents, and none indicate to a modern reader which valleys and rivers were being referred to. Chichilticalli for example consisted of a tumbled-down house without any roof, made of red earth—an archeological ruin—somewhere in an unsettled part of southeastern Arizona. A consensus on this general location seems to be unanimous. The building was large and appeared to have been a fortress, built by people who came from the north. This immediately suggests a late prehistoric adobe structure built by a group whom archeologists call the Salado. Somewhat farther south, the Spaniards attempted to establish a settlement at several places now referred to as Corazones I, II, and III, the first two at least being in what is now far northern Mexico. Corazones III, the final location of the presumptive town the Spaniards named San Geronimo, lay on a little river in the Valley of Suya, fifty leagues north of Corazones I. Native rebellions at two of these sites left many settlers dead and drove the rest away.

Where to place any of these names on a modern map has been a guessing game, somewhat like searching for the Lost Dutchman Mine. People from all walks of life—anthropologists, historians, military officers, geographers, churchmen—have added confusion with their arguments over possible locations. They have often made tentative identifications of 16th century locations based on one referent while ignoring others.

At best, there is general agreement that the Rio Nexpa was probably the San Pedro River. This river was mentioned only in the later narrative by Juan Jaramillo, however, not by Fray Marcos, Pedro de Casteñada, or Coronado. Francisco Vásques himself, in his letter of August 1540 to the viceroy, passed over in silence anything about his route from Las Corazones—well-down in northern Mexico—to Chichilticalli, and Jaramillo was explicit that "just a few Indians came out to see the general" impliedly as the Spaniards arrived at the Rio Nexpa, somewhere below Chichilticalli. If Fray Marcos had indeed followed a "valley very heavily settled by people" in his earlier journey, what had become of these people when the Coronado *entrada* came through a year later? The captain-general put this discrepancy down to gross exaggeration by the priest. Is it possible that the friar and the general might have followed different valleys when they entered the Southwest?

In addition, both Fray Marcos and the authors of the Coronado-related documents left the Indians along the route unnamed, an omission that appears almost inexplicable. A century later, that part of modern Arizona and adjacent northern Mexico was the country of the Cipias and Ipotlapigas. By the 1690s, the Indians along the San Pedro River were called the Sobaipuris, and the unsettled people east of them were labeled the Janos, Jocomes, and Sumas.

Any creditable decisions as to Coronado's route across southern Arizona must depend upon the discovery of new information. And new information does keep turning up. In 1999, publication of the last will and related documents from a soldier who died in New Mexico during the expedition added the names of eight European members not found in any previously-studied records. Significant omissions should also be noted. Fray Marcos did not even mention a river, much less assign a name to one, citing his location of "this valley very heavily settled..." at least five times simply as "this valley," from whence it was four days' travel to the beginning of the second *despoblado*. The Valley of Suya was named only by one later writer, Pedro de Castaeñda, not by other chroniclers.

Period artifacts are now known from the Jimmy Owens Site in Blanco Canyon near Floydada, Texas, a major Coronado campsite on the High Plains. This site was found in 1993 and has gradually been excavated and yielded chain-mail fragments, crossbow bolt-heads and many other Coronado-period artifacts, but there is no consensus as to which of the two longer-term camps mentioned in Castanada's account of the trek across the plains this site might represent.

One recent book, *The Coronado Expedition to Tierra Nueva* (1997), concluded that interest was higher than ever, but scholars have had very limited success in agreeing on the route of the *entrada* in Arizona. In the absence of new sources, fresh perspectives on the information we do have may be helpful. For example, on August 3, 1540, Coronado wrote to the Viceroy from Cibola that he set out from Chichilticale and entered the [second] wilderness on Saint John's Eve. Saint John's Day would have been June 24, 1540 (Julian calendar).

He mentioned no river, only that during the first days he "found no grass, but rather a worse mountain route and more dangerous passes, ...with [no] relief from the previous difficulties." In his narrative written in the 1560s, the soldier Juan Jaramillo tells us that he came to a river they called Saint John [San Juan] "because we reached it on his day." Jaramillo we know traveled with Coronado's advance party. This river apparently lay three days' march beyond the foot of the mountain range "where we were told it was called Chichiltically." Jaramillo however was often unsure about distances and directions, which he blamed on a memory overtaxed by the long years since the expedition. Francisco Vásques' statements are less specific, but they are contemporary with the events, and probably serve to discredit Jaramillo with respect to Chichilticalli and the several streams he named.

Coronado noted that he arrived at the Red House and rested there for two days, because their horses were worn out. Others commented on the vegetation change there, where the "spiny forest" [i.e. cacti, mesquite, acacia] was left behind. This would account for the horses being in poor condition, but why the Spaniards then forged ahead into a landscape evidently lacking forage is difficult to understand. It also would seem to preclude their having crossed the Sulphur Springs Valley, which should have been a grassy paradise for horses and livestock at that period. The probable explanation is that we simply lack important information, either because of significant omissions in the contemporary records or as a result of failing memories in statements made later. A better policy, instead of relying upon selected bits of information, would be to compare everything that bears upon vegetation changes, topography, the possible locations and appearance of named places, rivers, and native groups encountered. This may be easier said than done, but still lies within reason.

Another new perspective is gained if we scale the distances between the seven named places from Culiacán to Cibola. Scattered through the documents are distance figures between most of these places, expressed in leagues. Each day's march was paced and also estimated, so these distances weren't arbitrary guesswork. If you line up these named locations across a sheet of paper and write in the number of leagues between them, two by two, using the numbers given in the narratives, you find that many distances are consistent and the overall length of the march was 300 to 310 leagues. Coronado himself gave the distance as 300 leagues. You can add or subtract to derive distance measurements not expressed directly.

Working these out, Chichilticalli can be seen as lying about 200 to 210 miles south of Cibola—eighty leagues at 2.63 miles per league. This places it somewhere along an arc between Casa Grande on the west, and south of Apache Pass on the east, well south of Eagle Pass or the Safford-Pima, Arizona, area favored by historians, which is only sixty-five leagues from Cibola. Other references such as days of travel, directions, and distances have all failed to narrow down the location of Chichilticalli because the only reference point firmly identified lies at the very end of the route, the historic Zuni Indian pueblo of Hawikuh at Coronado's Cibola.

To backtrack for a moment, Juan Jaramillo's account had the expedition marching four days through an unsettled land (*despoblado*), then two days downstream along the Rio Nexpa, thence "Once we left the stream, we went to the right to the foot of the mountain range in two days of travel, where we were told it was called Chichiltically." Fray Marcos had said that it was four days' journey *from* a well-settled area to the second uninhabited region, although his report did not use the name Chichilticalli. He asserted that they travelled on from "this valley," indicating no direction. Jaramillo's narrative included at least two erroneous directions towards the northeast, and his are the only statements as to how the expedition proceeded from the Nexpa to Chichilticalli.

Reconstructions of the route that have relied on Jaramillo include one by Betty Graham Lee who suggested that Chichilticalli lay in the Eagle Pass area at a site she excavated there, while archeologist Emil Haury thought that the ruin might have been on the slopes of the Pinaleño Mountains between Eagle Pass and Bonita, Arizona. But if Jaramillo's directions were wrong, there is nothing otherwise to support the Eagle Pass location.

Since 2006, an entirely new approach initially offered promise for identifying the trail. A geologist, Nugent Brasher, proposed a route and tentatively identified a series of campsites that have yielded metal artifacts that he believes to be of the period of Coronado's *entrada*. These include a possible crossbow bolt-head, iron nails and tacks and fragments of these, lead musket balls, copper-alloy aglets, broken bits of horse tack, a medallion, and other items. These were recovered by using metal detectors at the Kuykendall Site, a late prehistoric ruin in the Sulphur Springs Valley, heavily vandalized during the last century, and at possible camp locations to the north in present-day New Mexico.

Although Brasher is confident that the Kuykendall site is Chichilticalli, the basis for his identification is not clear. It is the only known Salado site in the Sulphur Springs Valley, but nothing he found there unquestionably supports his claim and other students are skeptical. This site was partially excavated by two amateur archeologists, Jack and Vera Mills, in 1951–1961. They reported clearing some 160 rooms and recovering 175 cremation burials. Historical artifacts are not mentioned. Two archeomagnetic dates, of A.D 1385 +-23 and

A.D. 1375 +-18 years are reported. Many of the rooms had been vacated prior to their having been burned. The site location had been occupied historically in the early twentieth century as a homestead, and heavily disturbed by farming and earthmoving activities prior to the Mills' work. The prehistoric rooms were built of adobe and arranged in a series of compounds, far exceeding the single room or unit described for Chichilticalli. The landscape surrounding the site originally was Sacaton grass. Brasher's artifacts were not recovered by controlled excavations and few if any of these necessarily date from earlier than the homesteading period. A late 18th century Spanish coin was found.

Brasher's research evidently continues and his proposed camp locations and the route between these, to where the trail leaves Arizona at the head of Doubtful Canyon on the Arizona—New Mexico border, needs to be confirmed by independent researchers. All in all, the geographical references in the sixteenth century documents appear to be at wide variance with this newest proposal. The segment of the indicated route from the Kuykendall Site to Doubtful Canyon is easily drivable in a pickup truck were it not for fence lines—hardly "a worse mountain route" so-called by Coronado. His straight-line distance from Chichilticalli to Cibola, repeatedly stated to be eighty leagues (about 213 miles) is very close to the measured distance of 218 miles, however. Kuykendall is the only large Salado site in this part of southeastern Arizona and is probably much too large to be Chichilticalli.

So, after 480-odd years, some answers to the puzzle over Coronado's route across Arizona are beginning to come to light. These don't depend upon insights gained from horseback rides, conferences, or the discovery of new documents, but from looking for evidence on the ground and also realizing that what has survived in the hodgepodge of records must be carefully compared. One researcher noted aptly that Chichilticalli when found should have an abundance of artifacts as clearly attributable to the Coronado *entrada* as those found at the Jimmy Owen Site. The sixteen horsemen under Melchoir Díaz and Juan de Zaldívar sent northward in November 1539, after the return of Fray Marcos, spent a good part of the winter in the vicinity of Chichilticalli and returned to meet up with the north-bound Coronado expedition. A stay of this length should have left at least as much debris as was found at the Jimmy Owens Site. Nothing of this sort is known from any place in Arizona. New routes are being proposed, but until we have better information, nothing can be confirmed. Perhaps when all is done, even the monument at Lochiel, Arizona, that supposedly marks where Fray Marcos de Niza entered what is now the United States, may see its claim confirmed.

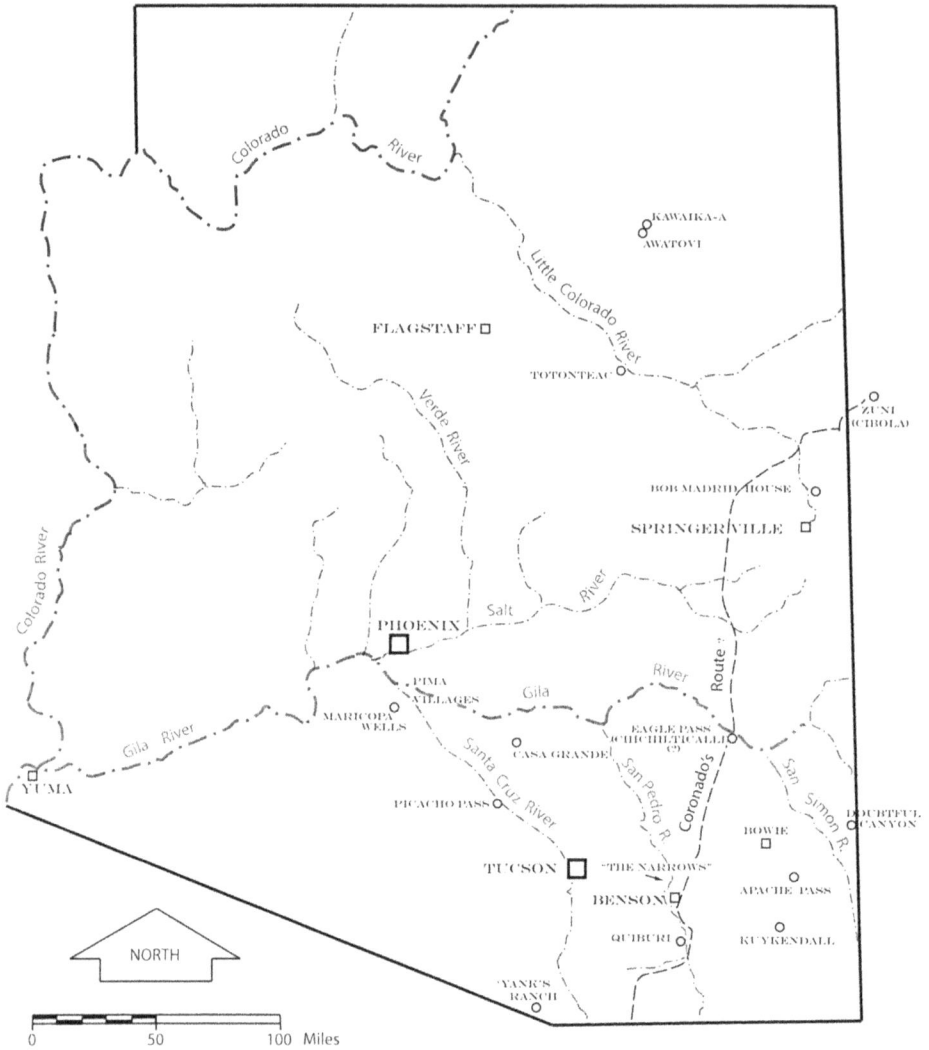

Some locations for Arizona Episodes. (Map courtesy of the author)

Francisco Vásques de Coronado.
(Courtesy Carson County Square House Museum, Panhandle, Texas)

Captain López de Cárdenes discovers the Grand Canyon.
(Courtesy of Harry Anderson, artist)

REFERENCES

Background for this article can be found in the following:

Articles by Nugent Brasher in *The New Mexico Historical Review* beginning in Vol. 83 No. 4 (Fall 2007).
Chichilticale.com. website by Nugent Brasher.
Chichilticalli, Coronado's Proposed Eastern Route. website by Andy Ward.
Flint, Richard, and Shirley Cushing Flint. *The Coronado Expedition to Tierra Nueva: The 1540–1542 Route Across the Southwest*. Niwot: University Press of Colorado, 1997.
Flint, Richard, and Shirley Cushing Flint. *Documents of the Coronado Expedition, 1539–1542*. Dallas: Southern Methodist University Press, 2005.
Haury, Emil W. "The Search for Chichilticale," *Arizona Highways* 60:4 (April 1984) pp. 14-19.
Lee, Betty Graham. *The Eagle Pass Site: An Integral Part of the Province of Chichilticale*. Safford: Eastern Arizona College Museum of Anthropology Publication No. 5, 1996.
Mills, Jack P. and Vera M. *The Kuykendall Site, A Pre-historic Salado Village in Southeastern Arizona*. El Paso: Special Report Number Six, El Paso Archaeological Society Inc., 1969.
Simpson, Brig. Gen. J.H. "Coronado's March in Search of the Seven Cities of Cibola and Discussion of Their Probable Location." Washington, DC: *Annual Report of the Smithsonian Institution for 1869*, pp. 309-340. 1871.

An earlier version of this article appeared in the December 1999 issue of *Arizona Senior World*.

2

THE FIRST CORRALS IN THE SOUTHWEST

Narratives by early Spanish explorers include many details about the first two corrals built in the Southwest. From their accounts we learn who built them and where, when and why, what materials were used, and their size. In one case we even know where to look for the remains. Both corrals date from the late sixteenth century and each was a remarkable feat of construction.

Antonio de Espejo with fourteen soldiers and a Franciscan friar left northern Mexico in November 1582, and by the first of February 1583 the party had made its way up the Rio Grande into New Mexico as far as the first pueblos in the Piro Indian country, just below latter-day Fort Craig. They spent almost a month among the pueblos along the Rio Grande, then headed west to visit Acoma and the Zunis. From Zuni they decided to go on to the Hopi Indian villages, partly because they had begun to hear rumors of mines. On April 17, 1583 (in the Julian calendar) the Spaniards plus an escort of eighty Zuni warriors " ...travelled six leagues and halted in the province of Mojose [Moqui, or Hopi], at a pueblo that had been attacked and destroyed by Coronado. ... It was and is situated a league from the pueblo of Aguato" [Awatovi].[1]

Historian Baltasar de Obregón, writing in 1584, also claimed that one of Coronado's captains, don Pedro de Tovar, "had destroyed a city in this province called Tuzayán to avenge the death of five Christians killed by the natives." He did not name the destroyed pueblo and the Coronado narratives are silent about this event.[2]

In any event, the people of Awatovi turned out to meet Espejo, bringing more than enough food for all. Obregón added that "They [the Spaniards] arrived at sunset. At this hour the natives came to receive them a league beyond their town."[3]

The campsite was said to lie a league from Awatovi and at an abandoned pueblo, which should have put the explorers near the ruins of Kawaika-a, situated along the southern edge of Antelope Mesa, three and one-half miles northeast of Awatovi. If Kawaika-a was destroyed by Tovar, its occupation extended beyond the archeological Pueblo IV period (A.D. 1300–1500) to 1540 or 1542. The linguistic affinity of this pueblo is uncertain.

April 18, 1583 saw the planning, construction, and total service life of the first corral in the Southwest! Of these events we have no less than three contemporary accounts. Espejo himself said only that

"We gave them [the Hopis] some presents of little value, which we carried, thereby assuring them that we would not harm them, but told them that the horses which we had with us might kill them because they were very bad, and that they should make a stockade where we could keep the animals, which they did."[4]

Diego Pérez de Luxán, the diarist of the expedition, tells us more: "We asked them to build a stockade of dry masonry in which to keep the horses, because the friendly Indians [the Zunis] told us that we could not trust these people. It was built this same day, which was Thursday the eighteenth" [of April].[5]

Luxán thoughtfully omitted any mention of Espejo's little deceit, whereby he gained the Hopis' labor. Finally, Obregón gave the most complete details. Although not a member of this expedition, he alloted their exploits considerable space in the near-contemporary history that he completed in April 1584:

> "It should be noted that on the following day [April 18] the people of Ciboro [Zuni] suggested that the Christians should build a fortress and that they would help. This was done with the aid of the people of Ciboro and Mohoce. The fortress was built of stone, about one *estado* high, more or less. Thus the surrounding land could be seen at a glance. Its walls were two *varas* thick. It was over 60 yards square, with only one entrance through which two mounted men could ride abreast. There were so many people to build it that it was finished in four hours. It was of no use to them because they decided to go to the pueblo called Aguato, which was visited by the captain and nine soldiers."[6]

An *estado* is equivalent to 1.85 yards, or about the height of a man. Assuming that Obregón's dimensions were approximate and rounding off a bit, the Indian labor force should have laid up some 847 cubic yards of masonry, exclusive of any interior walls, in this four-hour period. The natives must indeed have been willing workers. Espejo wrote that more than 2,000 Indians came out to welcome them, which gives credence to the claim that they accomplished so much in such a short period.

The Spaniards' horses, ten at least and probably with spare animals, must have had comfortable quarters that night. On Friday morning the whole troop moved to Awatovi and their corral was forgotten. No later narratives mentioned it, until archeologist J. O Brew penned his summary of the Peabody Museum's 1939 Awatovi expedition field season. He listed "the excavation of a newly-discovered Spanish building which seems to have been a stable and barracks" and published a plan of the structure, but did not describe it or link it to the Espejo expedition.[7]

More recently, historian James Brooks has unraveled the story of Awatovi's destruction by other Hopis in the fall of 1700, a violent episode in which no Spaniards were involved. Brooks wrote that a structure came to light in the far northeastern corner of the site during Peabody Museum's work. This he called an unfinished, even hastily abandoned effort to build a military barracks/stable. It measured some 150 feet wide and 120 feet deep, "with stalls for a dozen horses and barracks for an equal or greater number of soldiers."[8]

Brooks attributed this construction to Franciscan friars, impliedly to Father Fray Juan Garaicoechea, who had begun the construction of a new mission church at Awatovi in the spring or summer of 1700. Although Obregón's dimensions of the fortress or stockade were considerably larger than those shown on Brew's archeological plan and the location lay much closer to Awatovi than to Kawaika-a, the historian was not writing from first-hand knowledge and it would appear that Brooks' military barracks/stable is actually Espejo's corral, built some 117 years before the Spaniards returned to Awatovi in 1700. It is probably the earliest example of Spanish construction in the Southwest, perhaps in North America, and is amazingly intact.

The second corral-building episode took place at the opposite end of the Southwest in October 1598. Don Juan de Oñate and the first permanent settlers of New Mexico arrived during the summer of 1598 and established their headquarters by San Juan Pueblo [now called Ohkay Owingeh]. The colonists soon set about exploring the new country and receiving obediences from the various Indian pueblos. On September 15, Oñate sent *Sargento Mayor* Vicente de Zaldívar Mendoza and some sixty men to the buffalo plains. As Oñate put it,

"I sent my *sargento mayor* to find and utilize the buffalo to the east, where he found an infinite multitude of them, ..."[9]

Oñate's buffalo were what we now call bison.

Two weeks after starting, the troops found themselves among the buffalo and the plains Apaches. Finally, on October 8, 1598, "...they went on three leagues farther in search of a good location for a corral and the materials with which to build it. Having located a site, they proceeded to build a corral of large cottonwood logs, which took them three days. It was so large and had such long wings that they thought they could enclose 10,000 head, because during those days they had seen so many cattle and they roamed so close to the beasts and the horses."[10]

Gaspar Pérez de Villagrá gave us the names of the men involved in this operation. The motive obviously was to capture some of the animals

"The sergeant major, wishing to capture a few of these buffalo to take back to the pueblo of San Juan that the rest might see them, ordered a great stockade to be built."[11]

However, the buffalo had other ideas.

"The corral being completed, they set out the following day toward a plain, where, on the preceding afternoon, they had seen about 100,000 head of cattle. As they rushed them, the buffalo began to move toward the corral, but in a little while they stampeded with great fury in the direction of the men and broke through them, even though they held close together; and they were unable to stop the cattle; because they are stubborn animals, brave beyond praise; and so cunning that if one runs after them, they run, and if one stops or moves slowly, they stop and roll, just like mules, and after this rest they renew their flight. For a few days the men tried in a thousand ways to drive them inside the corral or round them up, but all methods proved equally fruitless. This is no small wonder, because they are unusually wild and fierce; in fact, they killed three of our horses and wounded 40 others badly."[12]

No buffalo ever saw the inside of the Spaniards' corral. The would-be buffalo herders, probably tired and very frustrated, next took to capturing buffalo calves. This they could do, but the calves were no less fractious and none could be brought within a league of camp alive, whether dragged or carried on the horses, "for all died within little more than an hour."

The great buffalo corral experience technically ends here, and Zaldívar's party returned to San Juan on November 8. A few loose ends remain, and these can be pursued in order to round out the story. One question is the motive or motives for capturing buffalo in the first place. Villagrá said they wished to bring a few back to San Juan. However, there is also this interesting sentence in the narrative, made with reference to the calves: "...so it seems that unless they are caught soon after they are born and mothered by our cows or goats, they cannot be taken until the buffalo become tamer than they are at present."[13]

Hammond and Rey suggested that the underlying idea was to capture some animals with the idea of domesticating them.[14] The sequence of events and the wording of Zaldívar's report tend to support this explanation. It didn't work then, and after this experience the Spaniards evidently dropped the whole idea, since we have no evidence that they ever tried it again.

Another problem is the location of this corral. There is a daily record of the distances traveled, and the use of cottonwood logs would necessarily place the structure near a sizeable watercourse. Historian Herbert Bolton inferred that the troops were near to or beyond the present New Mexico-Texas border and close to the Canadian River.[15] He was probably correct, and these suggestions are the closest determination we can make of the actual location.

Finally, why did the Spaniards decide on the use of a *corral* for trapping buffalo? The best explanation seems to be that this was a technique familiar to them from Mexico, where they had presumably used similar corrals for rounding up cattle. The only early reference to a southern plains group possibly using such a device is a one-sentence entry in Gaspar Castaño de Sosa's journal. On November 23, 1590, his party had reached a point somewhere northeast of present-day Orla, Texas, along the Pecos River, below the New Mexico-Texas border, where

"A very large corral was found which the Indians used to enclose stock" (*ganado*).[16]

The modern editors of the journal inferred that this was a game trap and so it may have been, but the narrative itself tells us nothing more.

In fact, while the records of the Coronado, Chamuscado, and Oñate-period *entradas* into the Great Plains all describe the dependence of the plains Indians on the buffalo, their accounts are almost completely silent on the Indians' hunting techniques. Perhaps this detail was overlooked because it was obvious to all present on these expeditions. The Spaniards, with their guns and horses, clearly had no trouble riding or walking within range and shooting the animals down. The only two comments on what the Indians did were included in descriptions of Zaldívar's 1598 trip:

"Their weapons consist of flint and very large Turkish bows. The Spaniards saw some arrows with long bone tips, although only a few, as the flint is better for killing the cattle than the spear. They kill them at the first shot, with amazing skill, while hiding in brush shelters built at the watering places, as was witnessed by all those who went there."

Again, "The Indians kill them with arrows at their watering places, make dried meat from them, and take their tallow and fat."[17]

Lying in wait by the water hole was a perfectly good method, especially considering the Indians' lack of both horses and firearms at this early date. Whether other hunting procedures were in use, such as pounds and drives, we simply do not know. Sites of prehistoric bison drives are recorded from Colorado, the Texas Panhandle, and especially the southern plains, so the drive was practiced by some plains groups whether or not the Apachean peoples knew of it. The available evidence only suggests that Zaldívar's corral was more likely modeled on prior experience in Mexico than on anything observed among the local Indians. If so, could the pounds or traps observed among plains and Southwestern Indians 200-plus years later have been a result of Spanish influence, rather than an old native technique?

Corrals had a rather spectacular introduction to the Southwest. Of the hundreds or thousands which the Spaniards, Indians, and Anglo-Americans built during the ensuing centuries, probably few if any were as pretentious as these first two or used for anything much more glamorous than as holding pens for cattle, sheep, and other domestic livestock.

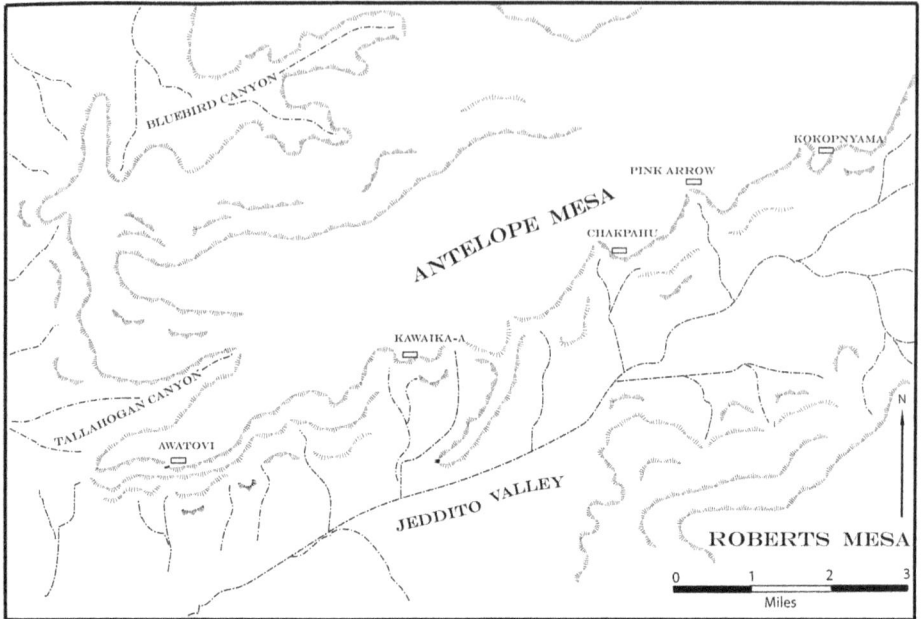

Antelope Mesa and Awatovi.
(Map courtesy of the author)

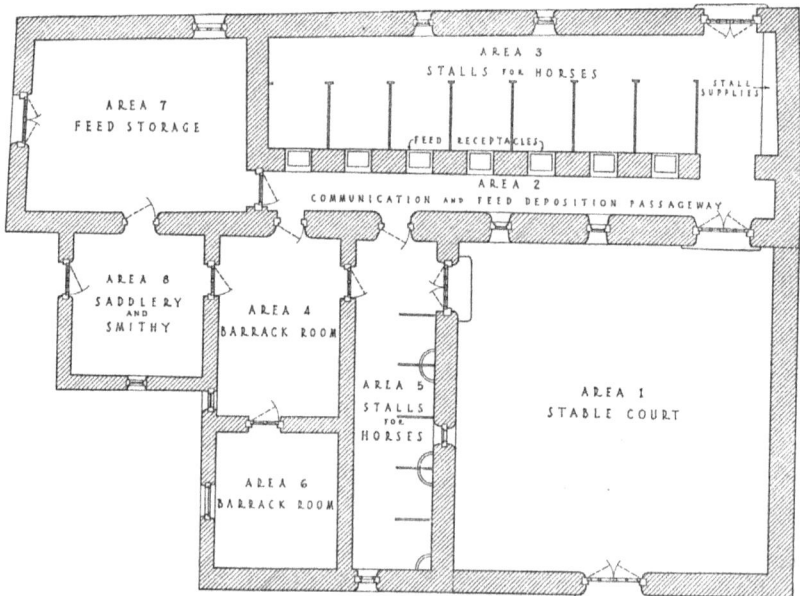

Espejo's Corral or Stable at Awatovi. (Courtesy of the Peabody Museum of Archaeology and Ethnology, Harvard University, PM 2004.1.123.1.1779)

Notes

1. George P. Hammond and Agapito Rey (trans. and eds.), *The Rediscovery of New Mexico, 1580-1594*, pp. 188-189. Coronado Cuarto Centennial Publication 3. Albuquerque: University of New Mexico Press, 1966.

2. George P. Hammond and Agapito Rey (trans. and eds.), *Obregon's History of 16th Century Explorations in Western America*, pp. 327-328. Los Angeles: Wetzel Publishing Company, Inc., 1928.

3. Hammond and Rey 1928, p. 328

4. Herbert Eugene Bolton, *Spanish Exploration in the Southwest, 1542–1706*, p. 185. New York: Barnes & Noble, Inc., 1908 (reprinted 1967),

5. Hammond & Rey 1966, p. 189.

6. Hammond & Rey 1928, pp. 328-329.

7. J.O. Brew, "Preliminary Report of the Peabody Museum Awatovi Expedition of 1939." *Plateau* 13:3 (January 1941), p. 42.

8. James F. Brooks, *Mesa of Sorrows: A History of the Awat'ovi Massacre*, p. 215. New York: W.W. Norton & Company, 2015.

9. Bolton 1908, p. 215.

10. George P. Hammond and Agapito Rey (trans. and ed.), *Don Juan de Oñate, Colonizer of New Mexico, 1595-1628*, p. 401. Coronado Cuarto Centennial Publications 5-6. Albuquerque, University of New Mexico Press, 1953.

11. Gaspar Pérez de Villagrá, *History of New Mexico* (translated by Gilberto Espinosa), pp. 156-157. Los Angeles: The Quivira Society, 1933 (reprinted 1962).

12. Hammond and Rey 1953, pp. 401-402.

13. Hammond and Rey 1953, p. 402.

14. Hammond and Rey 1953, p. 18.

15. Bolton 1908, p. 227.

16. Albert H. Schroeder and Dan S. Matson, *A Colony on the Move: Gaspar Castaño de Sosa's Journal, 1590-1591*, p. 62. Santa Fe: School of American Research, 1965.

17. Hammond and Rey 1953, pp. 404, 640.

3

AWATOVI—NEW LIGHT ON A LEGEND

One northeastern Arizona perennial revives whenever a historian, archeologist, or ethnologist contributes some new piece of information. The perennial is the "Awatovi legend," the sequence of events that culminated with the destruction of this early historic Hopi Indian pueblo, allegedly in the late fall of A.D. 1700.

Early-day archeologist Adolph Bandelier published the first summary account of Awatovi's violent end.[1] This prompted another archeologist, J. Walter Fewkes, to place on record a traditional Hopi version plus the inferential support he drew from his own archeological explorations at Awatovi.[2] Missionary H.R. Voth recorded more Hopi traditions,[3] and in 1949 another archeologist, J.O. Brew, utilized the available historical documents to elucidate the history of Awatovi as understood at that time.[4] Watson Smith subsequently reviewed the 17th century missionary establishments among the western Indian pueblos, including Awatovi,[5] while Christy Turner and Nancy Morris documented a mass burial site discovered on the bank of Polacca Wash as a probable massacre of Awatovi villagers.[6] More recently, historian James Brooks has given us his reconstruction of the events at Awatovi.[7]

For an affair that took place more than 300 years ago, in the absence of literate witnesses, to find among the disparate sources such agreement as to what happened is a rare pleasure. One can compare Bandelier's and Father José Narváez' versions, the latter written in 1732, with each other and with other published traditions, add in the bits of archeological evidence, and find the parts mutually supporting.[8] Where history and native traditions do not agree, it is over the motives that impelled Hopis from other villages to kill most of the Awatovi males, abduct the women and children, and destroy the village. The probable truth may be the historical version that has the apostate Hopis resentful of an

Awatovi willingness to receive back the friars and permit renewed missionary activities, as of A.D. 1700. Awatovi and the other southwestern Indian pueblos had been relieved of any Spanish presence since the Pueblo Revolt of 1680.

The weakest link in the reconstruction of events is the historical record; no known *contemporary* documentation has survived and the only primary source cited by recent scholars has been Father Narváez' 1732 account. Narváez was an old-timer, acquainted with the religious and soldiers who had entered the Hopi country since Governor Diego de Vargas' reconquest in 1692-1693, but his synopsis was penned long after the events had taken place. This doesn't mean that his veracity should be questioned, only that the documentary support is awfully thin. Bandelier didn't see Narváez' description until long after 1892, but he did have a 1722 document. This in turn hasn't been seen since Bandelier's time, but it may turn up again. Bandelier's version[9] must be based on this 1722 archive and there is no reason to doubt that he effectively summarized its contents as these related to Awatovi.

Totally elusive and most exciting of all is a collection of testimonies dating from 1713, recorded in a 1713 inventory of the Santa Fe archives.[10] The loss of Awatovi cost the Spaniards their foothold with the Hopis and was a slap in the face as well, so an official investigation—the collection of testimonies—would be predictable. Such had been made regarding the loss of New Mexico following the 1680 Pueblo Revolt. The body of information from 1713, if it existed now, could settle our questions about what happened at Awatovi. Diligent searching might yet produce fragments of this fat package (63 *fojas*) or perhaps official copies of the records within it.

The nearest thing to a contemporary reference has been a January 20, 1702 letter from the *Cabildo* of Santa Fe that detailed the "vigilant care and devotion" of Governor don Pedro Rodríguez Cubero, and mentioned as well that "During the months of June and July of last year, 1701, the governor campaigned against the apostate Indians from the province of Moqui. He punished their daring and their treacherous actions against the converted Indians of Awatovi Pueblo, where, based on his long experience, he carried this out with great zeal."[11] If our other versions are substantially correct, Cubero's accomplishments were vastly overstated in this letter.

A real puzzler is the absence of any comment on Awatovi's end in Fray Silvestre Vélez de Escalante's excellent history of New Mexico, the *Extracto de Noticias*,[12] composed around 1778 and for which Bandelier used the misleading citation—Escalante, *Relación*. This did include an account of the efforts at conversion and negotiations with the Hopis up through October 1700, but his story then jumped to early 1701 and Cubero's expedition, giving no reason for the latter. Vélez de Escalante clearly didn't know the whole story—nor did he find the 1713 testimonies, which may already have disappeared from the Santa Fe archives.

The Biblioteca Nacional in Madrid contains the seventeenth-century equivalent of a service record for Juan Domínguez de Mendoza, a citizen-warrior who one historian characterized as the most distinguished soldier in seventeenth century New Mexico. The record is Ms. 19258, *Servicios personales del Maestre de Campo Don Juan Domíngues y Mendoza*, a series of certifications dating from and subsequent to his long term of active service, ca. 1640–1690. He fled south with the other survivors of the Pueblo Revolt in 1680 and in 1683-1684 led a famous expedition into west Texas from El Paso.[13] Later he went to Spain and died there in a hospital, about the time Governor Vargas finally reestablished the authority of Spain over New Mexico.[14]

However, the latest document in this file is dated September 18, 1701, at Santa Fe, and once again we find the valorous conduct of Juan Domínguez de Mendoza attested! The occasion was Governor Cubero's campaign to the Hopi country. The old soldier, who had "appeared to be sixty years of age, a little more or less" in October 1684, couldn't have been the combatant this time around, and other items in the collection show that he had two legitimate sons—Balthasar, aged 25 as of October 1684, and Juan, then a few months shy of 20. Presumably it was Juan Jr. who returned to New Mexico and at the age of 36 received an official certificate, eventually deposited in his father's file. Since the present article was first printed in 1972, historian Marc Simmons has published the entire Domínguez de Mendoza service record.[15]

The 1701 attestation presented here is brief; a complete transcript is given below together with an English translation. It has three main points of interest that touch on Awatovi: (a) it is the earliest known primary statement on the loss of the pueblo and it agrees with Bandelier's dating of the event; (b) it confirms the timing and purpose of Governor Cubero's subsequent campaign against the other Hopis and, by significant omission, implies that this expedition accomplished little; (c) the remarks about Awatovi, if rather brief, agree with the sequence of events describe by Bandelier and Father Narváez. The legend begins to look very solid.

To the Biblioteca Nacional and Sr. Tomás Magallon Anton I am indebted for a copy of the document, and to Ms. E. Boyd of the Museum of New Mexico I say thank you for correcting and improving my translation. The proper name of the individual is Domínguez *de* Mendoza, although the *y* is occasionally used, as in this document.

El Castellano Dⁿ Pedro Rodriguez Cubero, Gou^{or} y Capitan general de las Provincias del Reyno de la nueba México por su Magestad, &c^a

Certtifico al Rey nfa S^{or} en la Real audiencia de la Ciudad de México, y demas Jueces y Justicias de su Magestad, como en la campaña que ejecuté por los meses de Junio y Julio en la Provincia de Moqui contra los Yndios Apostatas della, sobre la aniquilación que hicieron en los Yndios convertidos del Pueblo de aguatubi, se hallo en dicha function con riesgo manifieste de la Vida Dⁿ Juan Domínguez y mendoza, llebando asi cuidado y por su Quenta todos los bastimentes y pertrechos para la guerra que se les hizo, sin que en medio de tanto enemigo y rodeado que se hallaba perdiere cossa alguna de lo que tan nesesario llebaba, baliendose de las experiencias que tiene del Reyno, y peleando con todo es fuerzo y Valor como bien Vasallo de su Magestad, como todo fué publico y notorio a todos, y para que consté donde conversa y a fabor de dho Dⁿ Ju-Dominguez y mendoza doy la presente en esta Villa de santa fee en dies y ocho dias del mes de septiembre de mil setecientos y una, firmada de mi mano y sellada con el sello de mis armas, y refrendada del presente secretario.

Pedro Rodriguez
    Cubero (rubric)
        Por m^{do} del Sor Gou^{or} y Capp_____ral
        Pedro de Morales (rubric)
        S^o de Gou^{or} y Gue^a

***

The *castellano* don Pedro Rodriguez Cubero, governor and captain-general of the provinces of the kingdom of New Mexico for his Majesty, etc.

I certify to the king, our lord, through the royal *audiencia* of the City of Mexico, and the other judges and courts of his Majesty, on the matter of the campaign which I carried out during the months of June and July in the province of Moqui against the apostate Indians there, following the annihilation which they committed upon the converted Indians of the pueblo of *Aguatubi*; it happened in this engagement, with manifest danger for the life of don Juan Domínguez y Mendoza, transporting thus with care and by his own account all of the provisions and munitions for the war which was made against them, surrounded and in the midst of so many enemies, that it was done without anything being lost of all which was so urgently needed and borne in, he availing himself of the competence gained through experience in this kingdom and fighting with all his might and with the valor of a worthy subject of his

Majesty, as was public and notorious, known to all. And for that I have placed on record what he reports, and in the favor of the aforesaid don Juan Domínguez y Mendoza I certify in this *villa* of Santa Fe, the eighteenth day of the month of September, the year one thousand seventeen hundred and one, signed by my hand and sealed with the seal of my arms, and counter-signed now by the secretary.

Pedro Rodriguez
Cubero (rubric)
By command of the governor and captain-general
Pedro de Morales (rubric)
Secretary of Government and War.

NOTES

1. A.F. Bandelier, *Final report of Investigations Among the Indians of the Southwestern United States, ...Part II*, pp. 368-373. Cambridge: John Wilson & Sons, 1892.

2. J. Walter Fewkes, "A-wa'-to bi: An Archeological Verification of a Tusayan Legend." *American Anthropologist*, Vol. 6 (O.S.) pp. 363-375. Washington DC, 1893.

3. H.R. Voth, The Traditions of the Hopi. *Field Columbian Museum Anthropological Series*, Vol. VIII. Chicago, 1905.

4. R.G. Montgomery, Watson Smith, and J.O Brew, Franciscan Awatovi: The Excavation and Conjectural Reconstruction of a 17th-century Spanish Mission Establishment at a Hopi Indian Town in Northeastern Arizona. *Papers of the Peabody Museum, Harvard University*, Vol. XXXVI, pp. 12-25. Cambridge, Mass., 1949.

5. Watson Smith, Seventeenth-Century Spanish Missions of the Western Pueblo Area. *The Smoke Signal*, No. 21. The Tucson Corral of the Westerners, 1970.

6. Christy G. Turner II and Nancy T. Morris, "A Massacre at Hopi." *American Antiquity*, 35(3) pp. 320-331. Washington DC, 1970.

7. Brooks, James F., *Mesa of Sorrows: A History of the Awat'ovi Massacre*. New York: W.W. Norton & Company, 2015.

8. Bandelier 1892, pp. 371-372. C.W. Hackett (ed.), *Historical Documents relating to New Mexico, Nueva Vizcaya, and Approaches Thereto, to 1773*, Vol. III. Carnegie Institution of Washington, Pub. No. 330 Vol. 3, pp. 385-386. Washington, 1937.

9. Bandelier 1892, p. 372.

10. Bandelier 1892, pp. 372-373.

11. John L. Kessell, Rick Hendricks, Meredith D. Dodge, and Larry D. Miller, editors, *A Settling of Accounts: The Journals of don Diego de Vargas, New Mexico, 1700–1704*, p. 63. Albuquerque, University of New Mexico Press, 2002. See also J. Manuel Espinosa, *Crusaders of the Rio Grande* pp. xv, 380. Chicago: Institute of Jesuit History, 1942.

12. Vélez de Escalante, Fray Silvestre—"Este cuaderno se cree ser obra de un religioso de la provincial de Santo Evangelico," in *Documentos para servir a la historia del Nuevo México, 1538-1778*, pp. 324-459. Madrid: Ediciones José Porrúa Turanzas, 1962. This is the incomplete version, first published in 1856, of Vélez de Escalante's *Extracto de Noticias*. There is a photostatic copy of the complete manuscript in the Library of Congress.

13. Bolton, Herbert Eugene (ed.), *Spanish Exploration in the Southwest, 1542–1706*, pp. 311-343. New York: Barnes & Noble, Inc., 1908, reprinted 1967.

14. Fray Angélico Chávez, *Origins of New Mexico Families, in the Spanish Colonial Period*, pp. 25-26. Santa Fe: The Historical Society of New Mexico, 1954.

15. France V. Scholes, Marc Simmons, and José Antonio Esquibel, *Juan Domínguez de Mendoza: Soldier and Frontiersman of the Spanish Southwest, 1627–1693*. Albuquerque: University of New Mexico Press, 2012. See pp. 286-287.

An earlier version of this chapter appeared in *Plateau,* Vol. 44 #3 (Winter 1972).

4

Fort Yuma: Hottest Post in all Creation?

Although Yuma, Arizona is warm and pleasant in the winter, it can be very toasty during the summer months. Indeed, this reputation extends back 170 years or so, almost to its beginning as a military post on the lower Colorado River, as we see from an old Army anecdote.

At the end of the Civil War in 1865, nearly all of the volunteer officers and men who served in the Union army were gradually mustered out. A year passed and Colonel James F. Meline expected to receive his discharge too, but before this happened, he somehow wangled a summer-long tour of the West, what we would now call a junket. This had no better object than to allow him to gather material for writing a travel book. He did write a book and it was a good one— *Two Thousand Miles on Horseback: Santa Fe and Back* (New York: Hurd and Houghton, 1868; reprinted by Horn and Wallace Albuquerque NM, 1966).

Colonel Meline never made it as far as Arizona, but he did learn some interesting things about the territory from men who had served there. One night around the campfire, three days from their arrival in Denver, the soldiers were discussing the comparative merits, or more likely demerits, of the various posts where they had seen service.

Which was the coldest post? The several candidates offered up were all routed, as the colonel put it, by a cavalryman who had wintered at Pembina, in the northeasternmost corner of what is now North Dakota.

Which is the hottest post? was the next question, and several stations in Florida and the Texas gulf coast had their advocates. But the subject was closed by an old sergeant, stone-faced and just as solid in his convictions:

"Boys, did any of you ever hear of Fort Yuma?" Not one of them had.

"Well Fort Yuma is clear over beyond Arizona, near the Gulf of California, where nothing lives, nor grows, nor flies, nor runs. It's the hottest post, not only in the United States, but in all creation, and I'll prove it to you"

"You see, I was ordered to Fort Yuma six years ago, and hadn't been on duty two weeks, in the month of August, when two corporals took sick. They had been there ever since the post was a post—in old Heintzeman's time [1850]. Well, they both died, and where do you think they went?" No one could imagine.

"Why, I'll tell you: they both went straight to hell!" Profound astonishment in the audience.

"Yes, but they hadn't been gone forty-eight hours, hardly time to have their descriptive lists examined and put on fatigue duty down below, when one night at twelve o'clock the hospital steward at the fort was waked up in a hurry, and there he saw the corporals standing by his bedside."

"'What do you want?' says he. 'What do you want?'" Hospital stewards, now called orderlies, had the reputation of always being out of temper at soldiers' wanting anything.

"'We want our blankets,' says they!"

"After that, you needn't talk to me about any post being as hot as Yuma!"

And silence hung around the campfire like a blanket.

Fort Yuma on the Colorado River, 1852. (Sketch by John Russell Bartlett)

5

Tucson As It Was in 1858–1861

For the years just before the Civil War, much of what we know about Tucson is to be found in California newspapers. These accounts of Arizona's only city (population 622 in 1860) were, as one paper put it, not always of a very flattering kind. Nor did the occasional correspondents who passed on the Overland Mail stages offer any more generous appraisals.

One anonymous writer commented when he reached Tucson on November 5, 1858, that while the town lay surrounded by mountains with bold and rugged slopes, it had a wretched, miserable look as one approached it. The buildings were all one-story and built of adobe, with flat roofs of thatched willow and cane. Six years later, author J. Ross Browne betrayed the same hint of bias by saying that the best view of Tucson was the rear view on the road to Fort Yuma. The 1858 correspondent also commented that shallow wells yielded excellent water, although everything there seemed to shake with chills and fever from attacks of ague. Presumably this meant malaria. Nor was this all, for the people went around armed to the teeth:

> "The knife is the law, and the revolver justice. Apaches are constantly prowling around the environs, seeking life or plunder; and the inhabitants are constantly on the watch, ... Every person here seems afraid of the smallest bush."

Things had not improved much by 1861, when the first number in a new series of the Tucson *Arizonian* newspaper appeared on February 9, 1861 and added its own cautions to potential visitors

"Tucson enjoys a reputation throughout the country by no means enviable. This is demonstrated by the extreme precautions taken by timid passengers in the Overland coaches, who betray their apprehension of danger in watchful glances and constant vigilance. Some will not traverse the streets without a pistol in hand, ready for any emergency. But while these are only evidences of gross exaggerations relative to the actual state of society here, we have a reality far from agreeable to lovers of law and order. Deadly weapons are drawn on slight and frivolous occasions, and bloody fights are almost as common as polemics in the halls of Congress. We have, too, a class of the *Bombastes Furioso* stripe [i.e., loudmouthed braggarts] who are loud in their boasts of valor, but who...though causing no bloodshed, contribute greatly toward the ill name which attaches to Tucson. And the fair name of our metropolis is further tarnished by the hilarious displays of visitors from the rural districts, who seek recreation for a season in the excitements of city life."

And lastly, the same paper commented one month later on the sad state of city planning, not to mention zoning, in Tucson:

"We observe many houses in process of construction this spring in Tucson. For the most part, the buildings are erected helter-skelter, without regard to streets or convenience."

Today's travel writers, the literary descendants of these early correspondents, write instead of master planned communities, graceful retirement living, golf lovers' packages, the city's natural beauty and amazingly pure air, and Tucson's unique character. On this last point and particularly the visitors who sought recreation in the excitements of city life, Tucson today does offer variety and spontaneity. Fortunately, its attractions now are mostly not what a correspondent in 1861 would have had in mind.

Tucson from the Southwest, 1852. (Sketch by John Russell Bartlett)

REFERENCES

Browne, J. Ross. *Adventures in the Apache Country*. Tucson: University of Arizona Press (1974 reprint), page 138.

Daily Alta California (San Francisco), September 17, 1860, page 1.

Daily Evening Bulletin (San Francisco), November 5, 19, 1858.

Los Angeles Star, February 16, 1861, page 3.

The Ranchero (Corpus Christi, Texas), November 3, 1860, page 1.

The San Francisco Herald, February 21. 1861, page 3; March 21, 1861, page 1.

6

Early Days of Newspapering in the Southwest

Newspaper journalism in southern Arizona dates from 1859 and in southern New Mexico to 1860. *The Weekly Arizonian* at Tubac and Tucson reflected the interests of its silver-mining owners, while *The Mesilla Times* in Mesilla, New Mexico, represented a closely-knit group of land promoters. Still another venture, the *Mojave Dog Star*, appeared October 1, 1859 at Fort Mojave on the Colorado River, with the ostensible object of correcting the free love tendencies of the Mojave Indians. Or so a correspondent of an Arizona paper claimed years later.

These pioneering sheets and particularly those that succeeded them found plenty of room for editorials and news stories written, as one historian put it, "in direct, vigorous, personal style with considerably more editorializing than present tastes allow."

Most papers had a publisher, an editor, a printer and a printer's assistant or 'devil' to do the actual production. No other staff was needed, and much of the content was simply reprinted from papers published elsewhere that had come to hand through exchanges. Local news typically appeared on a single page, and paid advertisements were sought as eagerly as they are today. On the other hand, outside criticism could bring an eloquent response from a thin-skinned editor, as when the *Arizonian* replied to an imagined slight by the *Santa Fe Weekly Gazette* by stating that the latter was "long known as a brazen puffing-machine for a clique of contractors and certain army officers." The target of this barb, a Santa Fe trader and New Mexico Superintendent of Indian Affairs, published the *Gazette* as well. Such charges sometimes lit off editorial feuds that reached heights of expression and absurdity that left their readers vastly amused.

While a few early newspapers were actually hand-written, the *Arizonian* and *Mesilla Times* came off of Washington hand presses; massive and virtually indestructible pieces of Yankee ironwork that printed one sheet at a time with hand-set type. Both presses still survive, one at the Tubac Presidio State Historic Park Museum in Tubac and the other at the Palace of the Governors print shop in Santa Fe. Within their own realms, editors and publishers exercised their rights as opinion-makers with little restraint, while volunteer correspondents occasionally filled the role of reporters. However, it was another matter entirely when members of the public entered a newspaper office. An 1858 number of the *Los Angeles Star* listed the rules that applied then.

"Printers' Rules – The following rules have been unanimously adopted by the 'craft,' and are expected to be observed:

1. Enter softly.
2. Sit down quietly.
3. Subscribe for the paper.
4. Fork over what you owe.
5. Don't touch the poker.
6. Say nothing uninteresting.
7. Engage in no controversy.
8. Don't touch the type!
9. Keep six feet from the table.
10. Don't talk to the printers.
11. Hands off the manuscript.

Gentlemen observing the rules when entering a printing office will greatly oblige the printers and need have no fear of the devil. The ladies who sometimes bless us with their presence for a few moments, are not expected to keep the rules very strictly, and it will be agreeable to us to have them break the ninth rule as often as convenient. Boys, unless accompanied by their parents, are particularly requested to keep their hands in their pockets."

Washington Hand Press at Tubac Presidio State Historic Park Museum, Arizona.
(Photograph courtesy of the author)

Washington Hand Press at the Museum of New Mexico, Santa Fe.
(Photograph courtesy of Museum of New Mexico)

REFERENCES

Los Angeles Star, May 1, 1858, page 1

The Weekly Arizonian, April 21, 1859, page 2

McClintock, James H. *Arizona: Prehistoric, Aboriginal, Pioneer, Modern*, Vol. II pp. 501-502. Chicago: The S.J. Clarke Publishing Co., 1916.

Kenneth Hufford, "Journalism in Pre-Territorial Arizona," *The Smoke Signal*, No. 14. The Tucson Corral of the Westerners, 1966.

John P. Wilson, "Does the Museum Own the Original Mesilla Times Press?" *El Palacio* 78/3 (1972), pp. 10-13.

7

JEFFERSON DAVIS' RAILROAD DREAM
BECOMES A MAIL LINE TO CALIFORNIA

In 1880 and 1881, two transcontinental railroads linked New Mexico and Arizona to the rest of the United States. This could have happened twenty years earlier if the U.S. Congress had allowed itself to be swayed by the efforts of one of its members.

In the late 1850s, an ambitious scheme to link the eastern United States with the Pacific Coast was floated in the U.S. Senate. Early in 1858, the Senate Select Committee on the Pacific Railroad reported out a bill to authorize the President to contract for the transportation of mail, troops, and other government services by railroad from the Missouri River to San Francisco. At that time, there were no railroads between Missouri and California. A few senators raised some questions, but for almost a year nothing happened. Looking back, we can see that one senator had something special in mind.

In January 1859 a serious debate on the question of a Pacific Railroad began. By the middle of the month, senators began to complain that this issue now consumed half of their time. The prospect of the government even becoming involved was answered by the timeless justification that a railroad was needed for national defense. California lay separated from the rest of the United States by a largely unsettled country, and any foreign threats remained vague or imaginary.

The desirability of such a railroad was not seriously questioned, but its location immediately became a sensitive issue. Should only a single route be surveyed, or as many as three routes? The secretary of war in 1859, a Virginia man, had already gone on record that the 32nd parallel or desert route from El Paso, Texas, to the Colorado River and southern California, had "very decided advantages" including (in his words) sufficiently abundant water. Other possible locations, usually called the central and northern routes, lay as far north as present-day Wyoming and Montana.

Jefferson Davis, then a prominent senator from Mississippi and a member of the select committee, had served as Secretary of War during the government-sponsored Pacific Railroad Surveys in the early-middle 1850s. That monumental study had provided the best available information for deciding where a railroad might best be built across the western United States.

Davis was thoroughly familiar with these volumes, but equally so was Senator Henry Wilson from Massachusetts, who favored a central route. In the debate, they quoted at length with respect to a 32nd parallel route, cherry-picking their information. The Massachusetts senator cited any number of reports whose authors claimed that western Texas from the Pecos River to El Paso was barren and worthless, and the country beyond as far as San Diego was sterile and barren. Neither a sprig of grass nor a drop of water was to be found in a dry, parched-looking plain, destitute of trees, with almost unendurable heat in the summer months.

Senator Davis viewed the same landscape as a country of easy grades, where good tie-timber and lumber could be obtained from the local mountain ranges; where the arid areas would be made fertile by water from artesian wells (an earlier Davis scheme). He claimed that the longest intervals without permanent water amounted to forty miles or less, and the pace of road-building would be limited mainly by the speed with which ties and rails could be delivered and laid. Little preparation of the natural surface was needed. In an amendment, he asked for an appropriation of $10 million and ten sections of land per mile to construct a railroad between the states of the Atlantic and the Pacific. He might as well have asked for the moon.

While most of the senators simply sat and listened, Jefferson Davis finally owned up to what everyone else already knew; he favored a 32nd parallel route for the railroad. He did not exactly claim that this land flowed with milk and honey, but he warned that the more northern routes should be avoided as sterile and impracticable, and in doing so he referred to one senator as "My friend from the hyperborean region of Iowa." Hyperborean? Iowa? Hawkeyes in parkas and mukluks? Perhaps when seen from Mississippi, or warmed by a dose of Southern Comfort.

The senators generally tried to play down any claim that the choice of location was a sectional argument—North vs. South. But the undercurrent was there, and the Massachusetts senator at one point accused a colleague from Georgia of "proposing to build a southern [rail]road, so that when the South dissolved the Union it would come within the southern confederacy." He proposed to call the 32nd parallel route the "desert and disunion route."

The Georgia senator had spoken about events that might lead to a separation or secession of southern states from the Union, and in this he was prophetic. There is a chilling message in these speeches from January 1859, in that the senators already realized that the time was not far distant when the Union would be dissolved. Although southern senators might approve of several locations for a Pacific railroad, any appropriation to build a line that lay outside of a southern confederacy and belonged exclusively to the North was unacceptable.

Finally, on January 27th the Senate voted on a bill to invite proposals for construction of a Pacific railroad along three separate routes. By then the debate had degenerated into a farce, as a senator from California put it, and it was obvious to all that the legislation was dead whether it passed or failed. It did pass, by a vote of thirty-one to twenty, as a version offered by Senator Andrew Johnson of Tennessee, with everyone exhausted and just wanting this behind them. The bill never made it to the House of Representatives. A similar proposal was revived in February 1861, this time with the princely sum of $125 million in thirty-year bonds attached, but several southern states had already seceded and the proposal went nowhere.

Even as the legislative effort for a Pacific Railroad died in the U.S. Congress, two overland stage lines were running along the southern route to California favored by Davis, now President of the Confederate States of America. Both crossed what is now southern Arizona. The Butterfield Overland Mail operated from September 1858 until Congress withdrew the heavy subsidy that supported it and authorized the Postmaster General to discontinue their contract on 2 March, 1861. Some stages continued to roll until early April.

There was also the San Antonio and San Diego Mail Line, which depended on another federal subsidy to provide mail and passenger service between San Antonio, Texas and San Diego, California. This had a very different history. It too continued running its stages until the spring of 1861, but soon after the Postmaster General annulled the Butterfield contract, he awarded George Giddings, the San Antonio and San Diego mail contractor, a *new* contract to link San Antonio and Los Angeles with his coaches. This contract, worth $175,000 a year, was to run from 1 April 1861 to 30 June 1865.

Acting on his new federal contract, Giddings returned from Washington to Texas by late March and began to put his operation in order. Henry Skillman had charge of the Western Division. He had enjoyed a long career as an express rider and stage-line operator himself, and now sought to reestablish and stock the old stations during April and May.

Quite apart from this, it appears that Confederate operatives were already at work. A wagon train travelling in company with one led by Washington Peck, *en route* from New Mexico to California, met up with "eight men on horseback with a pack animal, Southern Confederacy mail" eastbound between Kinyon's station (also known as Murderer's Grave) and Oatman Flat on the lower Gila River in western Arizona. This was on or about May 11, 1861, and from them the emigrant party learned of the fall of Fort Sumter and the beginning of the Civil War.

The San Antonio and San Diego company began regular stage service from San Antonio to Mesilla, New Mexico, by 1 June 1861, and mail from Tucson reached Los Angeles on 20 June. Operational details that have survived are almost nil, but Henry Skillman arrived at Mesilla with the first *California* mail on 10 June, six days from the Pima Villages, which lay just south of modern Phoenix. The distance was about 380 miles; not very good time for this run.

The second westbound mail departed from Mesilla on 18 June and by the end of the month newspapers reported that the San Antonio and San Diego line was in "complete running order" with bimonthly service between San Antonio and Los Angeles. Nothing was said about intermediate stage stations, although in earlier days two had existed, at Maricopa Wells and the San Simon crossing, both in southern Arizona. By mid-July, *weekly* mail service from California had commenced. This was short-lived, as the *Mesilla Times* reported in its "*Extra*" of July 29th:

> "An Express from Pino Alto brings the appalling intelligence that the mail bound for Los Angeles California, which left Mesilla on the 2?th, had been taken near Cook's Springs by the Apaches and the guard murdered. The Express passed Cook's Springs on the 27th, and found six bodies in the cañon near the Springs, stripped of their clothing, and three of them scalped. They had been killed several days. The coach was destroyed."

This became known as the Free Thomas party massacre, after the name of the conductor. The paper also gave the names of the six passengers killed and noted that all "were experienced frontiersmen, picked for the dangerous duty they had to perform, and undoubtedly gave the Indians a most desperate struggle."

Robert Doyle, superintendent of the Western Division based in California, managed to send a final mail from San Diego(?) through to Mesilla a week before the Confederate invasion of southern New Mexico on 27 July,

1861. This invasion meant that the largest part of the mail route (744 miles of approximately 1457 miles), the portion between San Antonio and New Mexico, lay firmly within the Confederate States of America, in addition to which Southern sympathizers largely controlled southern New Mexico and Arizona.

Under Giddings' contract with the Federal government, his San Antonio and San Diego Mail Line had enjoyed about a month of revived operation before Congress finally rescinded the contract in July 1861. But did this cancellation interfere with mail service? Not at all. George Giddings had accepted a *Confederate* Post Office Department contract in June to provide mail service between San Antonio and El Paso, their Route No. 8076. Ever the entrepreneur, Giddings saw no conflict in carrying the same mail for two governments already at war with one another, over the same route, while (hopefully) receiving payments from both. Then in August 1861 this "Mercury of the South" signed a new contract with Confederate postal authorities to carry mail from San Antonio to Los Angeles, twice a month, for $250,000 a year. This allowed his existing operation to continue, although he was now reduced to working for a single government.

All of this finally made sense of scattered newspaper references to Confederate mail riders crossing the Pima and Maricopa Indian reservation in southern Arizona. On 12 August 1861, Henry Skillman rode out of Mesilla with mail for California, escorted by Lieutenant Levi Sutherland of Coopwood's Spy Company (i.e. San Elizario Spy Company) and fifteen Confederate troopers. Sometime before 23 August they arrived in Tucson. This was probably the same San Antonio and San Diego mail that rode into Los Angeles the evening of 31 August. The couriers or express riders who carried it beyond Tucson probably did so without an escort. Skillman himself did not continue past Tucson, as he intended to withdraw the San Antonio and San Diego stock until Indian affairs had quieted. The Indian attacks reported by the Tucson *Arizonian* newspaper for 10 August indicated that this might be a very long time.

Although the removal of the mules and other property effectively shut down Giddings' mail line beyond Mesilla, someone made at least one more run to California, in September 1861. A letter from Los Angeles dated 20 September, published in a San Francisco newspaper, said that the last mail from the East had arrived there (Los Angeles) "the week past," and the service had been suspended.

But even this was not the end. Someone using the *nom de plume* "Selden" wrote from Los Angeles on 4 October, saying that a Mr. Reed "of the late SA & SD mail line" left Fort Yuma with some of his employees from Tucson on 24 September, bringing "advices" sent from Tucson on 18 September.

Without naming names, the writer of the Los Angeles letter indicated that someone had finally caught a whiff of Southern rascality, as they might have termed it, in the air of southern California. The correspondent referred to the revival of the San Antonio and San Diego Mail Line as "the hybrid mail," and he had strong reasons to suspect that "it has been the medium of constant intercourse between traitors here and rebels in Texas and the East. In other words, the mail, conducted at the expense of the Federal Government, belonged to the Southern Confederacy, and was used to forward their designs."[1]

The correspondent's suspicions were well-taken and only slightly out-of-date. When Giddings began his second contract with the Confederacy in August, the mail was *entirely* a Southern operation, no longer a "hybrid" one. According to Confederate Post Department records (now in the Library of Congress), the department officially curtailed its Route No. 8076 by November and listed Giddings as having received $135,000 of his $250,000 contract, presumably for six and one-half months of services. Whether the United States paid him through July is unclear.

The Confederate government appointed only two postmasters in far western Texas and the Confederate Territory of Arizona. One was at San Elizario, Texas, and we do not know the person's name. On 25 September, 1861, William D. Skillman, a brother of Henry Skillman, was designated postmaster at Mesilla, Doña Ana County, Arizona Territory, the only Confederate postmaster in present-day Arizona or New Mexico.

Whether or not Jefferson Davis took personal advantage of this mail service, others evidently did use it, paying either on the South's nickel or (before August) on Uncle Sam's. Belatedly, someone in Los Angeles got wind that the southern overland mail was a Confederate operation. When his letter appeared in the San Francisco newspaper, Federal authorities swiftly closed this window to the South, a "hybrid mail."

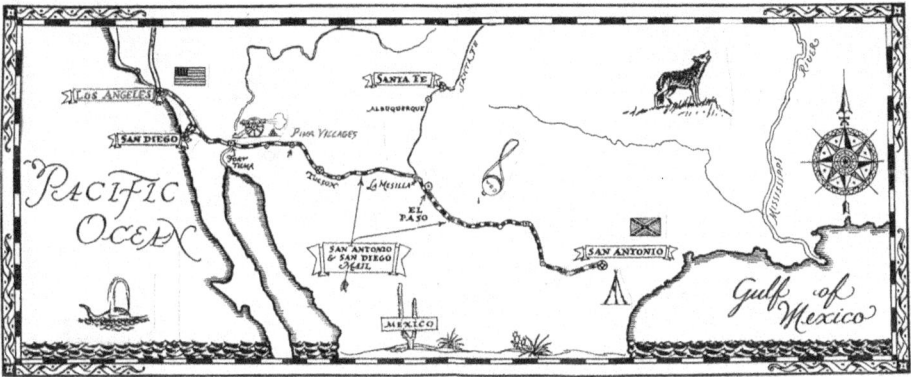

San Antonio and San Diego Mail Line to California. (Map courtesy of the author)

Confederate mail rider. (Original art courtesy of Jim Astholz, 2020)

NOTE:

1. Daily Alta California, 29 September, 8 October 1861.

REFERENCES

Austerman, Wayne R. *Sharps Rifles and Spanish Mules.* College Station: Texas A&M University Press, 1985.

Banning, Captain William, and George Hugh Banning. *Six Horses.* New York: The Century Co., 1930.

(The) Congressional Globe, 35th Congress 1st Session, Dec. 17, 1857–April 18, 1858.

Appendix to the Congressional Globe, 35th Congress 1st Session, page 35.

(The) Congressional Globe), 35th Congress 2nd Session, December 14, 1858–January 27, 1859.

(The) Congressional Globe, 36th Congress 2nd Session, February 13, 15, 1861.

Daily Alta California (San Francisco), Sept. 29, Oct. 8, Oct. 24, Dec. 17, 1861.

(The) Daily Picayune (New Orleans), October 19, 1861.

Erb, Susan M. *On the Western Trails: The Overland Diaries of Washington Peck.* Norman: The Arthur H. Clark Company, 2009. Also personal communication,Susan Erb, July 18, 2020

Los Angeles Star, July 20, 27, 1861.

(The) Memphis Daily Appeal, December 7, 1861.

Semi-weekly Southern News (Los Angeles), October 19, 1861.

Times–Extra (Mesilla, Arizona) July 29, 1861. Facsimile in *El Palacio,* vol.78/3(1972), 2.

An earlier version of this chapter appeared in the November 2000 issue of *Arizona Senior World.*

8

Scouting in the Chiricahuas: July 1864

In the summer of 1861, the oncoming Civil War prompted the withdrawal of all Federal troops from the two existing military posts in southern Arizona. Hostilities with the native Apache Indians had begun in February of that year, in consequence of the Bascom Incident in Apache Pass at the north end of the Chiricahua Mountains. With the soldiers now absent, citizens were left in a grinding war with the Apaches. It was the summer of 1862 before relief arrived with the arrival of a small army of California Volunteers, led by Brigadier General James H. Carleton, He left a garrison at Apache Pass that grew into Fort Bowie.

For a decade after its establishment, Fort Bowie was a major base for campaigning against hostile Indians. Expeditions into southeastern Arizona were initially made by the California troops, sometimes with local volunteers, who entered the field from Fort Bowie and another post, Fort Goodwin, on the Gila River. Carleton held overall command in both Arizona, which became a territory in its own right at the end of 1863, and New Mexico.

One of the early forays was led by Captain Thomas T. Tidball with twenty-five California Volunteers, which led to a bloody encounter with Aravaipa Apaches and many Indian casualties. This was in May 1863. General Carleton meanwhile had devised a strategy that involved sending four major expeditions against both Navajo and Apache Indians, beginning late in 1862 and continuing into 1865. The fourth and least-known of these was the Gila or Apache Campaign in the summer of 1864, mostly in the country along the Gila River. Captain Tidball led one of these scouts and his reports provided the first really good look at the upper Gila River Valley and the country north of it.

Tidball, just back at Fort Bowie from his month-long sortie along the Gila, set off once more in early July of 1864. This time he entered unknown country southeast of the fort and led his men into the Chiricahua Mountains. His guide was the scout Merejildo Grijalva, a Mexican captured by the Apaches in 1852, who remained with them for seven years and six months, during which time he became intimately familiar with their country. He escaped from them in 1859 and went to Mesilla, N.M., where he entered the employ of the government as a guide.

The captain's three-week reconnaissance covered more than 300 miles and employed part of his own Company K of the 5th Infantry, California Volunteers, and twenty-five men of the 1st Infantry, New Mexico Volunteers. His report, given here, gave readers an unprecedented description of the previously unknown Chiricahua Mountains and other parts of southeastern Arizona, at a time when it was still part of the Chiricahua Apaches' homeland.

It is unfortunate that no sketch map accompanied this report, as such maps were often included at this period. It would be more than a decade later, after the Chiricahua Reserve negotiated in 1872 between General O.O. Howard and the Apache chief Cochise was terminated in 1876, before outsiders had another look at the Chiricahua country. None of the place names that Tidball recorded ever found their way onto a printed map. The army's Atlas Sheet No 10, Parts of South-Eastern Arizona, published in 1878, may have been the first map to show any details of this country.

***

Head Quarters, Fort Bowie, Arizona,
August 8th, 1864.
Capt. Chas. A. Smith,
A.A.A. G. H'd. Qr's. Dist. of Arizona
Franklin, Texas.

Captain:

I have the honor to report that on the 10th of July I left this Post with a force of 60 men consisting of 2d Lieut. Juan C. Tapia and 25 men of Co. "A" 1st Inft. N.M. Vols., and 32 men of Co. "K" 5th Inft., Cal. Vols., and Berriguildi Grijalra (*sic:* Merejildo Grijalva), guide and interpreter. I took 22 days rations on pack mules and three in haversacks.

Sunday, July 10. – Leaving this Post, I marched in a S.E. direction along the foothills of the Chiricahua range on the S.W., camping in and examining the great cañons of these mountains. My first camp was a mile or so above the mouth of Carriso Cañon, about 15 miles by the trail from this Post. In this cañon I found good water by digging in the sand, in the bed of the arroyo. The valley of the cañon is about half a mile in width, with groves of oak and juniper, excellent grass and some patches of good soil. The upper part of it has perpendicular walls—impassible even for an Indian, and considerable pine timber was visible from our camp. A very heavy thunder storm in the afternoon prevented me from examining this cañon as closely as I desired. No trails cross the mountains through this cañon.

Monday, July 11. – Left camp at 5 o'clock, A.M., following my back trail to the mouth of the cañon, then bore to S.E. over rolling hills for four miles and entered Pino Cañon. I followed up the valley of this cañon two miles and found good water. The water rises in an arroyo and runs a short distance in several places, and then sinks. The water is permanent. This cañon has a large body of pine timber in the upper part and much of it can be reached by wagons without difficulty. I think that all the timber and lumber required for building the contemplated new post at this pass, can be obtained in this and Carriso Cañon. The transportation will not exceed 25 miles, and will be over an excellent natural road. An Indian trail crosses the mountains at the head of this cañon, and branches at the summit up and down the mountains on the N.E. side. At 6 o'clock P.M., a heavy thunder storm commenced and lasted until 10 P.M., raining very hard. By stretching our blankets over a frame work of willow rods stuck in the ground and bent and fastened together at the top, we managed to keep dry.

Tuesday, July 12. – Left camp at 7½ o'clock, A.M., travelling down the cañon the way we came to its mouth and then turned S.E. Passing over a rolling plain for several miles, I reached the "Cienegita," where my guide expected to find water, but it was entirely dry. From here the trail crossed a high, rolling divide and in about five miles entered the Tierra Blanca Cañon. I passed up this cañon about two miles, and finding a little rain water in holes in the rocks, encamped at 12 M. There was not water enough for my animals and I sent them two miles above where an abundance was found—rain water also. During the night a heavy rain furnished us an ample supply. My guide has always found permanent water here. There is some fine pine timber accessible in this cañon, and a large quantity at its head, possibly inaccessible without great labor.

Wednesday, July 13. – Left camp at 8 o'clock, A.M. Moving up this cañon about two miles, I sent the pack train with an escort over a low pass in the ridge separating this from the Cañon del Potrero, and proceeding up the cañon with the balance of the command for two or three miles, I turned south and crossed the divide into the Cañon del Potrero. I entered this cañon some four miles above its mouth, and in half an hour the pack train came up. I moved up the cañon two miles, and encamped at 12 M. Before we could prepare any shelter, a heavy thunder storm burst upon us and we got thoroughly saturated. There was a bold stream coursing through the cañon—greatly swollen now from rains. My guide says a little water runs in the upper part during the entire year. There had been much more rain here than at any point we had passed.

Thursday July 14. – Left camp at 7 A.M. following an old faint trail up the cañon, which grows narrower and the sides more precipitous as you ascend. Three miles above our camp the cañon branches—the main branch bearing round to the south and having numerous smaller branches. A good wagon road could be easily made to this point and a large body of timber reached. Pine and fir trees cover the entire region about the head of this cañon, from the bottom to the summit of the mountains. I followed the trail up the north branch, very rough and continually and rapidly ascending, about five miles—the last half mile exceedingly steep—and reached a high, sharp divide, from the summit of which we had a fine view of the Dos Cabezas, Apache Pass and the valleys to the north. The trail from here descended into the Tierra Blanca Cañon, in a northerly direction, and following up it for a mile ascends a steep mountain on the opposite side, there winds around the steep side of a high ridge to the S.W., and crossing the main ridge descends a few hundred yards into what is known as the "Potrero." Here I encamped at 1 o'clock P.M., men and animals very tired. This "Potrero" is an open grove of pine and fir trees free from underbrush, and covering an area of several miles, and is situated on an undulating slope on the eastern side of the mountain. A great deal of rain evidently falls here and the whole region is covered with grass, nutritious grass. A high ridge—probably the highest point in the Chiricahua mountains—borders this "Potrero" on the south and west. Along the base of this ridge are several springs of ice-cold water—the coldest spring water I ever saw. We found here wild strawberries, gooseberries, potatoes and onions. The mountains here for perhaps a distance of fifteen miles, are covered with a dense growth of pine and fir trees—from the summit down through the upper part of all the great cañons. This great body of timber must in time be very valuable to Arizona—especially in the event of a railroad from the Rio Grande to the Gulf of California. Much of the timber will be difficult of access but I have no doubt that when the demand will justify, capital and enterprise will reach it. This great timber region may have been examined and described heretofore by others who had more leisure and were better able to report it than I; but if so, I have never seen it and had no conception, until I visited it, of the existence of such a body of timber in these mountains. To me it is the most interesting portion of Arizona that I have visited. The change from ragged, barren mountains and monotonous plains is refreshing. There is no evidence that the Indians ever lived in the "Potrero." Berriguildi says they avoid it on account of the great number of bears which abound there. The trail over the mountains here is very faint and has not been used in a long time.

All the great cañons through which we passed, between this point and Apache Pass, were formerly favorite resorts of the Indians, as their numerous old "peels" indicate; but there is no evidence of their recent residence in any of them. I presume that none have lived there since the establishment of this post. The trails, though wide and formerly much used, showed no signs of recent travel. We found in one place, immediately upon a plain trail—in an old camp of the Mexican force which was up here in March last—a lance and bayonet; conclusive evidence that no Apaches had passed since.

Friday, July 15. – Left camp at 7 o'clock, A.M., traveling in a N.E. direction for about two miles through an open forest of pine. The trail which winds down the narrow ridge after leaving the "Potrero," bears to the S.E., and is faint and difficult to travel. We reached the foot-hills in about five miles, and struck a plain trail which runs along the foot-hills parallel with the mountains their whole length. I followed this trail for seven miles and reached the Rio Ancho, a rapid, rocky stream from twenty to thirty feet in width and from two to three feet in depth, and crossing to the south side, encamped at 1 o'clock P.M. A rain set in a few minutes after leaving camp in the morning and continued until after we encamped. This stream Berriguildi informs me, dries up at this point, but plenty of water can always be found a mile or two above in the cañon. It was now much swollen from heavy rains. The stream runs in the direction of the Cienega de Sauz, and is probably its main source of supply. There is most excellent feed here and an unlimited range, and it is altogether the finest location for an extensive stock ranch that I have ever seen in the territory. Timber in abundance along the streams and in the cañon.

About an hour after encamping, the guard with the herd discovered several Indians going up a steep mountain about a mile from camp. I immediately dispatched Sergeant Brown of Co. "K" 5th Cal. Vols., with 20 men in pursuit. Sergeant Brown and party went up the mountain very rapidly and, after passing a little the point where the Indians had been seen, was hailed, in Spanish, by an Indian from an almost perpendicular cliff about one hundred feet above them. He said he was a warrior and a brave man, and commenced shooting arrows. After throwing a few arrows without effect he began to throw rocks. He struck Corp'l Bair of my command with a rock and bruised his arm severely.

He soon fell mortally wounded and then called for Berriguildi, who he had recognized. When Berriguildi was satisfied he could not use his bow and arrow, he approached him and tried to get him to talk, but he would say nothing. He soon died. Berriguildi recognized him as an Apache chief named Old Plume, one of Chies' (Co-chies') old warriors, an Indian guilty of numerous murders and robberies, sullen and tyrannical among his own people and merciless to all others. He could easily have made his escape with the others, but he either halted to cover the retreat of his women and children, or else considered it unworthy a brave chief to run and with savage stoicism determined to sacrifice himself; in either case an act of heroism worthy of admiration even in an Apache. Serg't Brown suspecting that he had stopped to save his women and children, pushed rapidly up the mountain but owing to the nature of the place—it being almost entirely bare rock, and very broken and rough, he could not get their trail, and after several hours fruitless search returned to camp. There were five "Jacals" on the side of the mountain near the summit and several springs near them. The mountain itself is a bold bluff standing prominently out into the valley, and commanding a view of every possible approach from the valley. It would have been almost impossible to have surprised the Indians in this location. I named it Look-out Mountain. A mescal pit was found within four hundred yards of my camp, from which the roasted mescal had been drawn. This had been hastily abandoned by two or three women. It was a mere chance that we saw any of these Indians at all, as the heavy rains had obliterated all signs by which we might have detected their presence in the vicinity and prevented their mescal fires from being seen. I allowed the men to take what mescal they wanted, and had the balance destroyed.

Saturday, July 16. – Left camp at 7 A.M., following a plain trail along the foothills, near the base of a high bluff and rocky range of mountains on our right. After I had proceeded about four miles, the Indians were heard hallowing from the cliffs of this range. I halted the command and sent Berriguildi to have a talk with them, and instructed him to tell them to come into camp and make a treaty—assuring them that they should not be harmed if they would do so. After a parley of several hours four Indians came down to the edge of a grove about a mile from us, and one advanced to have a talk. He would not come near, and both were compelled to speak at the top of their lungs to be understood. The Indian said they would make a treaty and would come to the fort in eight days for that purpose. He said they belonged partly to Mangas' and partly to Chies' (Co-chies') bands, that they had a treaty and traded with the people of Janos, Chihuahua. Berriguildi insisted on their coming in and making a treaty now, which they finally agreed to do if I would encamp. I did not have much faith in their promises, but determined to test them, and moving forward a few hundred yards to a favorable location, encamped. Whether they had no intentions of coming in, or whether they feared treachery from a few of my men who had gone, without my knowledge, into a ravine merely for water, I do not know; but by the time the mules were fairly unpacked, they all fled up the mountain. An attempt to overtake them in their position was useless, and after an hour's delay I packed up and moved on. As soon as we moved, they commenced building signal fires along the cliffs in the direction we were going. I reached a "Laguna" in the edge of the Valley del Sauz, where my guide expected to find water, at 3 o'clock, P.M. but it was entirely dry. The signal fires convinced me there were more Indians in the direction we were going, and I was anxious to get forward as speedily as possible, but the necessity of having water compelled me to turn up the cañon to the right and seek it. I followed up this cañon about two miles and encamped at 4 P.M., without water. A rain in the evening afforded a supply.

Sunday, July 17. – Marched at 6 o'clock A.M., down the cañon and took the main trail. Discovered that two Indians had preceded us during the night. At 10 o'clock A.M. reached "Palm Springs," but found no water. After several hours' delay, scouts found water two or three miles up a cañon to the right, and I encamped at 1 o'clock P.M. Here I found several huts which had been occupied within a few weeks by a small party of Indians—but no fresh signs, the rain here as below having destroyed them. Satisfied that the Indians, if any in this vicinity, were on the alert, I determined to march that night and, if possible, get in the rear and surprise the rancheria near Rio Ancho. Accordingly, at dark I packed up and marched back, and encamped a 2 o'clock A.M. on the morning of the 18th in a cañon three miles south of where we had last seen the Indians.

Monday, July 18.- At day break I directed Lieut. Tapia with the main force and pack train to proceed leisurely down the trail to our old camp on the Rio Ancho, and if the Indians showed themselves to attract their attention as much as possible. At the same time, I started with Berriguildi and 20 picked men of my company up the mountain—hoping to get in the rear, or at least find them somewhere on the mountains. It is useless to attempt to describe the region we passed over. Suffice it to say that in all my experience in the mountains, not inconsiderable, I never passed over so rough and broken a region, or made as hard a march. The Indians had left, and owing to the rocky surface and heavy rains we were unable to tell in what direction they had gone. I am confident they were still somewhere high up in these cliffs, the rain supplying them with water and enabling them to occupy positions where they could not live in the dry season. I reached the Rio Ancho at 5 o'clock P.M., where I found Lieut. Tapia and command encamped. No Indians had been seen.

Tuesday, July 19. – Laid over. The stream had fallen somewhat and the water was very clear. Plenty of small fish show that this water is permanent.

Wednesday, July 20. – Left camp at 2 o'clock A.M. and marched back to my camp of the 17th, where I arrived at 10 o'clock A.M.

Thursday, July 21. – Marched at 3 A.M. – trail bearing to the S.W. Passed a high ridge in two miles from camp and entered the head of the Valley del Sauz, which here bears round to the south and west. In six miles reached a "spring," where guide expected to find water, but it was dry. Six miles further in a S.E. direction found rain water in a ravine, and encamped at 12 o'clock M. Shortly after encamping two Indians on horse-back were discovered following on our trail. They ascended a hill within fifteen hundred yards of camp, and called for Berriguidi. I sent him out with instructions to get them into camp if possible. They would not come within talking distance until he had brought his musket into camp. Finally, one came down—the other remaining as a lookout—and approached within seventy-five yards. Berriguildi recognized him as an old acquaintance named Ka-eet-sah. He asked what we wanted, to which Berriguildi replied that we wanted to make a treaty of peace with the Indians. Ka-eet-sah said they had made a treaty with the Mexicans at Fronteras, but that the Mexicans had broken it, and killed about thirty of them in one day—among them all of his family. He said there were no Indians in these mountains except the small band with him and the one at Rio Ancho—all under Old Plume. Ka-eet-sah asked what we went back to the Rio Ancho for—to which Berriguildi replied that we went back to send an express to the fort to tell them that the Indians would be there in eight days to make a treaty, and must be kindly received. He said Chies (Co-chies') was on the Gila with the Coyoteros. To an inquiry of Berriguidi as to what had caused the spring to dry up—he replied that it was in order that the soldiers could not follow the Indians; but afterwards gave a more satisfactory reason—that there had been no rain in that region for two years. He agreed to come into camp but wanted to smoke first, and requested Berriguildi to give him some tobacco. Berriguildi left him tobacco and returned to camp. He went back to his companion, had a smoke, and they mounted their horses and rode off very rapidly. Their principal object probably was to ascertain in what direction we were going. Berriguildi was greatly disgusted that I would not place men in ambush to shoot this Indian when he came down to talk. Satisfied that nothing could be done with these Indians at this time, I determined to cross the mountains and pass over to the Dragoon Spring range.

Friday, July 22. – Left camp at 3 (A?) M.—trail bearing N.W., through a wide cañon towards a low pass. I reached the summit of this pass in nine miles, the ascent being very gradual, and gradually descending about two miles, entered the great "Cañon de Aliso," and following down it in a S.W. direction, encamped at 12 M. We found good water—some in pools and some that ran a short distance and sank. An abundance of small fish indicate that the water is permanent. Permanent water is found on both sides of the pass, near the summit. The high mountains of the Chiricahua range terminate here—those to the south of this pass are lower and not so rough. Wagons could be taken through this pass without difficulty, and a little labor would make a road far superior to that through Apache Pass.

Saturday, July 23. – Marching at daybreak down the cañon, going S.W. for three miles to the valley. Trails from both sides of the mountains meet here and form one great trail to Fronteras, Sonora. Here the arroyo from the great cañon, which is marked by a belt of timber, turns to the N.W., and extends a long way out on the plain. Permanent water, I am informed, can be found in two places in the arroyo on the plain. Continuing S.W. over rolling hills for five miles we reached a divide, the waters from which flow into the rivers of Sonora on the south, and the Gila on the north. Near the summit, on the south side of this divide, is a spring of water in a deep arroyo, called "Alamo." Eight miles from here in a S.S.W. direction I entered a cañon in a great spur which curves out from the Chiricahua mountains and extends a long way to the N.W. down the valley. About a mile from the entrance of this cañon I found a little water in a hole, and by digging obtained plenty. I encamped here at 3 'clock P.M.

Sunday, July 24. – Left camp at 2 A.M. and passing down the cañon one mile reached the open plain. This cañon is narrow, but perfectly practicable for wagons, and the water is permanent. I struck across the plain without a trail in a S.W. direction, towards a gap in the Dragoon Spring range, and finding an abundance of rain water in pools on the plains in about 15 miles, encamped at 11 A.M.

Monday, July 25. – Marched at daylight. In six miles I struck a plain trail, bearing from the gap towards which I was traveling, to Sulphur Springs. A large band of cattle, mules and burros had been driven north over this trail very recently. I judged them to have passed at least forty-eight hours before, and deemed successful pursuit, with Infantry, impracticable. This undoubtedly is one of the greatest thoroughfares of the Coyoteros in their depredations upon Sonora. Following the trail, I entered the pass in four miles, and found a small spring about one mile from the entrance, in a ravine to the north of the main trail. There was not water sufficient for my command, and I went about two miles up a cañon to the right, and found plenty of water in a hole in the arroyo, but it was strongly impregnated with minerals and very unpleasant to the taste. We found here veins of alum or something very much resembling it. The whole appearance of these mountains indicates abundance of mineral. A very large band of Indians had wintered here—probably last winter. A heavy shower in the evening supplied us with good water.

Tuesday, July 26. – Marched at daylight and in two miles reached an open plain stretching down to the San Pedro river. Wagons can be taken through this pass easily, and could pass without difficult from the San Pedro over the route I traveled to the head of the Valley de Sauz, and the longest interval without water will not exceed twenty-five miles.

I was anxious if possible, to go down through the mountains to Dragoon Springs, and with this object in view left the trail leading to the San Pedro and struck into the mountains to the north. There was no trail, and after making an exceedingly hard march of fifteen miles, I was compelled to leave the mountains and go to the San Pedro—eight miles farther, when I encamped at 3 o'clock P.M.

Wednesday, July 27. – Laid over on the San Pedro.

Thursday, July 28. – Marched at daylight down the river and encamped at 11 o'clock A.M., at a point on the river about a mile from the San Louis Silver mine.

Friday, July 29. – Marched at daylight. Faint trail bearing N.E. over a barren, rocky mesa. In twenty miles I reached a marsh, where we attained good water by digging. This marsh is marked by four sycamore trees—the only trees save mesquite near there.

Saturday, July 30. – Marched at daylight and entered a cañon in the Dragoon Spring mountains in four miles. The ascent to the summit of the mountain on the N.W. is very gentle—on the N.E. it is very steep. After reaching the edge of the valley on the N.E., I traveled south and in two miles found water high up on the side of the mountain. Encamped here at 11 o'clock A.M.

Sunday, July 31.–Marched at 3 ½ o'clock, A.M. and striking across the valley to the south of Sulphur Springs–direct for this post. There was no trail. I found good water in holes about the center of the great valley. I encamped at 4 P.M. on the arroyo, marked by a line of green timber, which puts out on the plain about ten miles south of this post. I estimated my march thirty miles.

Monday, Aug. 1. – Marched at daylight and reached this post at 9 A.M.—having been in the field 23 days and marched something over three hundred miles.

I do not believe that a successful expedition can be made against the few Indians who now inhabit the Chiricahua mountains at this season. The heavy rains render it impossible to trail them, and destroy all the signs by which their presence is usually detected. They do not cultivate the soil, but live entirely by plunder and upon the natural products of the country. Their staple article is *mescal*, and during the spring and summer months, they are broken into small parties engaged in procuring their winter supply. Knowing that the smoke from the large fires which they require in preparing this food exposes them to observation, they are exceedingly vigilant. They are equally on the alert during the fall months when engaged in gathering mesquite beans and grass seeds on the plains. During the winter months they seek some timbered cañon, and unless short of food, generally keep close to their huts. Then, in my opinion, is the time to successfully operate against them. To insure success however, at least *two good scouts* are necessary. Berriguildi is thoroughly acquainted with these mountains, and perfectly familiar with the habits of these Indians; but he is constitutionally timid, and knowing as he does the terrible fate awaiting him if ever captured by the Apaches, he will not venture out of sight of the soldiers— or, if compelled to go, his statements cannot be relied upon, as he allows his fears to overcome his judgment and his regard for truth. In company with another good scout he would be very useful. In fact, every expedition should have *two or more scouts*—one to follow the trail, and the other to accompany him and watch the indications outside of the trail, prevent ambush and detect the presence of Indians.

The names by which I have designated the cañons, streams, &c., in the Chiricahua mountains are, according to Berriguildi, correct translations of those used by the Apaches.

I have the honor to remain, Captain,

Very respectfully,

Your obd't. serv't.,

T. T. TIDBALL.

Capt. 5th Inft., Cal. Vols.

Commanding Post.

Captain Thomas T. Tidball, 5th Infty., California
Volunteers, n.d.
(Photograph courtesy of the Santa Cruz,
California, Public Library)

Merejildo Grijalva, n.d.
(Photograph courtesy of the Arizona Historical
Society)

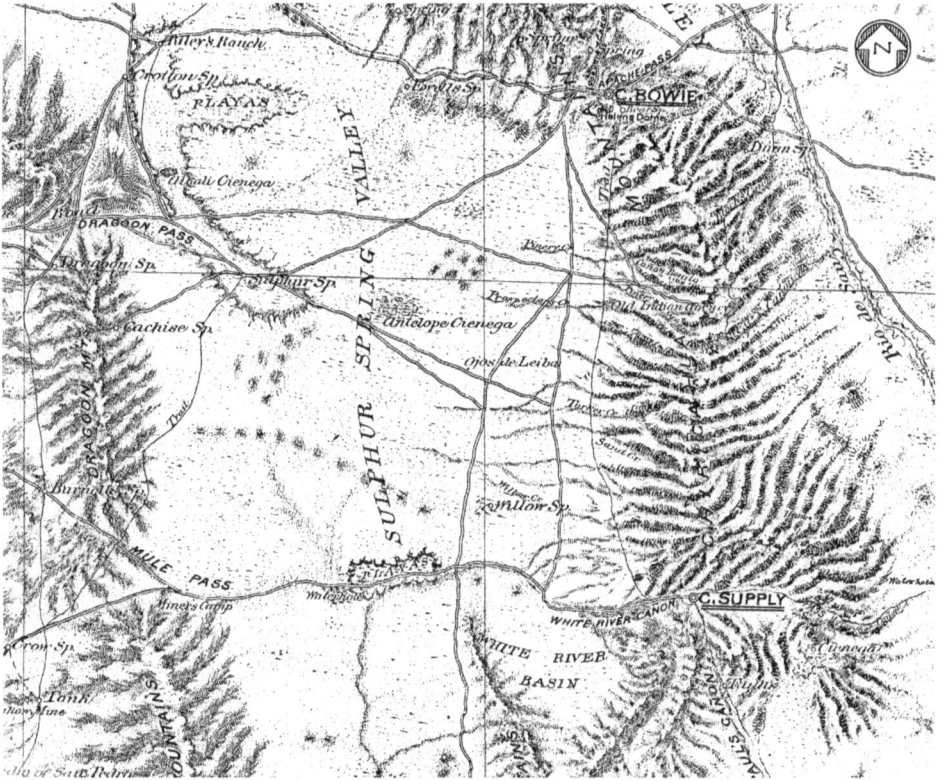

Detail from Parts of South-eastern Arizona; U.S. Army Atlas Sheet No. 10 (1878). (Courtesy of National Archives and Records Service, Record Group 77, Civil Work Map File, W275 Sheet 10)

REFERENCES

"An Apache Captive," in *The Arizona Graphic,* Vol. 1 No. 17, January 6, 1900. Phoenix, Az.

Santa Fe Weekly Gazette, October 15, 1864, page 2.

Sweeney, Edwin R. *Cochise, Chiricahua Apache Chief.* Norman: University of Oklahoma Press, 1991.

Sweeney, Edwin R. *Merejildo Grijalva: Apache Captive, Army Scout.* Austin: University of Texas Press, 1992.

Wilson, John P. *Islands in the Desert: A History of the Uplands of Southeastern Arizona.* Albuquerque: University of New Mexico Press, 1995, esp. pp. 95-98 and 107-113.

9

Stage Robbing—In the Buff?

One Saturday evening in early November of 1869, four would-be highwaymen had reason to regret their choice of a profession. Sixteen miles west of Fort Yuma on the Colorado River, a coach with six passengers and an express box rolled across the southern California desert, heading towards San Diego. Captain Shadrack Davis, a Wells, Fargo & Co. agent, drove the team because he expected an attempt to "jump" the stage. Alongside Davis on the box or driver's seat sat William Bichard, the post trader at Casa Blanca on the Gila River Indian Reservation in southern Arizona, holding a double-barreled shotgun.

As the stage started through a brushy ravine, Bichard remarked that "If we are attacked, it will be about here." Just then two men appeared in the road and one shouted for the stage to halt, while two others showed themselves to the sides. Bichard wasn't one to back down in a confrontation, as the Army and the Indian office learned two years later when they sought to remove him from the reservation. He immediately triggered his gun, which misfired, then fired the second barrel and gave one of the bandits a load of buckshot in the stomach. The robber threw up his hands and cried out, "My God, I am shot."

The fight commenced then as the outlaws blazed away, the passengers returning their fire. Bullets flew thick and fast; several shots struck the coach but the only other casualty was one of the horses. While passengers "skedaddled for the brush, in a lively manner," the so-called knights of the road retreated up the sides of the ravine. As soon as he could, Bichard headed back to the last station and returned with a reinforcement of four men. Although the attack happened at 8 o'clock P.M., enough light remained to recognize these robbers as having recently held up a Los Angeles-bound coach, after which they gambled away their loot.

Captain Davis continued on to the next stage stop, the Laguna Station, and there on Monday night he arrested one robber who gave his name as Frank Walker. Edibles and drinkables were scarce in the desert, and the following day two other men were taken into custody as they came towards that place, apparently starved out. The San Diego newspaper expressed its hope that a few of these fellows would soon dance at the end of a rope, which would make life and property safer in that part of the State. What became of Bichard's victim was not explained, or perhaps not known.

In a bizarre twist on this story, the first news report claimed that the "attack was made by four men, armed to the teeth and stripped to the buff." After they had been driven off, their coats and spurs were found hanging on the bushes. If they expected a lively fight, they got that and more, and only added to their problems by ensuring, as the *San Diego Union* put it, "that the robbers could be plainly seen."

REFERENCES

The San Diego Union, November 11, 18, 1869, both page 2.
Wilson, John P. *Peoples of the Middle Gila: A Documentary History of the Pimas and Maricopas, 1500s–1945*, 2014, chapters 11 and 12. Sacaton, Arizona: Gila River Indian Community, Cultural Resource Management Program.

10

ENCOUNTER AT PICACHO PASS

Thirty-year-old Samuel Drachman was 'electrified,' as he put it, by writer J. Ross Browne's tales of adventure in early territorial Arizona. These first appeared serially in *Harper's Monthly* in 1864–1865. In 1867, Sam set out from Philadelphia to join his older brother Phillip, who was already there. In a few years Sam would become a prominent Tucson merchant, but first he had to get to Arizona.

He took a ship to San Francisco, then proceeded to Los Angeles. With no stage service available beyond San Bernardino, he joined a well-armed party of men determined to push through to Arizona City, now known as Yuma. There at the Colorado River he managed to find passage on a buckboard carrying the mail to Tucson.

These were perilous times and Sam Drachman had heard that Indians along the Tucson road in particular had gone on the warpath, murdering people and stealing their stock, taking in stages and killing the passengers, with the situation only growing worse. A team of mules pulled the buckboard eastward along the old Butterfield Trail, changing animals at Oatman Flat and again at Blue Water Station.

Soon enough they got their arms and ammunition ready for the risky ride through "the Picach" or Picacho Pass west of Tucson. The driver began spinning stories, claiming that many a man had been laid low there. Their plan was to make this passage in the night. With his imagination fired up, every cactus, tree or bush appeared to Sam to be an Indian with a scalping knife in hand. He and the driver made ready to give them a warm welcome.

As they rolled into the pass, one of their mules was snake-bitten and soon could not even stand. The driver tried to extract the poison with a potent concoction of gunpowder and Jamaica Ginger, but this didn't seem to help.

Darkness came on and they decided against making a fire, since this would only draw Indians.

They pulled off the road and mused over their situation until around eleven o'clock, when they heard a low, murmuring sound and the tread of horses drawing closer. Indians! "Indians, sure enough," cried the driver; "let us do the best we can." Sam, a complete greenhorn, was in a state best imagined, as he confided later. The whispering sounds of human voices and approaching horses' hooves now sounded more clearly. He grabbed his rifle and made ready to fire. It turned quiet for awhile, and just as they expected to turn loose and sell their lives dearly, they were astonished by a clear, melodious voice, singing: "Hang Jeff Davis on a sour apple tree,"

Drachman's mind raced. "What's that? Surely these cannot be Indians!" He picked up the courage to raise his head. Indeed they were not, and by now the approaching party was close enough to be recognized as two well-known Tucsonians, Charles T. Hayden and Charles A. Shibell. Hayden, then a merchant, would become the father of Arizona's long-serving congressman and U.S. Senator, Carl Hayden.

The new arrivees pulled up and had a hearty laugh when told about the circumstances just past. After treating Sam and the driver to a drink of Arizona "bug juice," Hayden and his partner continued on, either oblivious to any dangers or more experienced about meeting them.

As Sam Drachman put it later, "Thus ended our anticipated Indian fight." The next morning their animals were much improved and they managed to reach Point of Mountain station. From there it was a short, relatively safe journey on to Tucson. Thirty years later, his fellow members of the Arizona Pioneers' Historical Society enjoyed Sam's story of how he came to Arizona.

Picacho Peak, 1864. (Sketch by J. Ross Browne)

Picacho Peak today. (Photograph courtesy of the author)

REFERENCES

Browne, J. Ross. *Adventures in the Apache Country,* Tucson: University of Arizona Press, 1974

The Arizona Graphic. Phoenix, November 18, 1899, pages 3-4.

Drachman, Roy P. *From Cowtown to Desert Metropolis.* San Francisco: Whitewing Press, 1999.

11

Two Young Heroes of Early Arizona

In the last months of Arizona's Indian wars, two ten-year-old boys saved their families from almost certain death. Geronimo and a few dozen Apaches had bolted back to Mexico after a failed peace conference in late March, 1886. Then in the early morning hours of April 27th he led an estimated thirty to forty raiders north again into Arizona, by a route far to the west of their earlier conflicts. They swept down the Santa Cruz River valley past Nogales and Calabasas, pillaging the ranches there before splitting into two bands. The Apaches that struck to the southwest apparently divided into smaller parties.

Early in the afternoon of April 28th, a Mr. J. Shanahan drove his grocery-laden burro past 'Yank' Bartlett's ranch in Bear Valley, about sixteen miles northwest of Nogales. He was bound for his own ranch, three miles away. Ten minutes after Shanahan left the Bartlett ranch, 'Yank's' young son Johnny heard three gunshots up the canyon and ran into the house to tell his father he thought the Indians had shot Mr. Shanahan. Bartlett Sr. said, "Get out of here, don't you get Injuns in your head like your mother." His mother fortunately was at Oro Blanco, a mining camp some nine miles to the northwest.

Johnny stepped out the door again when he heard Mr. Shanahan shout. The rancher carried no weapons and had tried to defend himself with rocks when the Indians shot him, front and back. Johnny and his father ran out 100 yards to bring Shanahan into the house and Bartlett now told his son, "Johnny, saddle your horse and go to Oro Blanco as soon as you can and tell the people Mr. Shanahan is wounded and that your father will be attacked in ten minutes."

Johnny saddled his mare and rode off as fast as he could. His father had told the boy to turn back if he saw Indians ahead of him. On a ridge about two miles from their house, three Indians came over the point of the mountain some 400 yards ahead. Two of them were swaying back and forth on their horses because, as it turned out, they'd gotten into the brandy at another ranch. They missed seeing Johnny, who turned around and headed back as fast as the mare could carry him. He heard the Indians firing as he neared the house, and when he galloped up to the front door his father ran out and lifted him off the horse just as they fired a volley. Right at this time, several bullets hit his father's saddle horse, who ran into the bedroom and fell dead.

Moments before this, Shanahan's young son Phil had been out looking for his father and passed below, down the canyon. 'Yank' noticed him coming back and yelled for him to run to the house. When Phil Shanahan saw his father badly wounded and groaning with pain, he started to cry. 'Yank' asked if he had seen any Indians at their house. He hadn't, so Johnny's father told him to crawl into the brush back of his own house, then go down the canyon until he got opposite a ridge and follow that to where he got in sight of the Shanahan's house. If no Indians were about, he should tell his mother that his father had been wounded and for her to take the children and hide in the canyon until dark, then bring them to the Bartlett's house.

Young Phil was crying "Mr. Bartlett, I can't do it," but 'Yank' told him "Phil, your mother and sisters will be killed by the Indians; you can save them!" The boy didn't want to leave his father, but he quit crying and replied "Well, if you think so, I will go" and ducked out of the house.

A little later, 'Yank' stepped out into the hall and looked around a corner to try and spot the Indians who were shooting at them. One of their bullets struck him in the shoulder, hit the adobe and filled Johnny's eyes with dirt, then glanced to within two inches of Shanahan's head. 'Yank' told his son that he'd been struck by a piece of adobe and more than an hour passed before the boy realized his father had been shot. The guns grew silent for a while, until 'Yank' spotted an Indian only sixty yards from the house and fired when he peeked over a big rock. The Apache then ran off up the canyon and climbed a tree. When he jumped out of the tree, 'Yank" fired again. The Indian threw himself on the ground among the brush and crawled off. Johnny noticed that he was wearing blue pantaloons with yellow stripes down the legs. Other Indians then began shooting at the house and kept it up until nearly sundown. Shanahan's family didn't appear.

In the meantime, little Phil had run first for the mountain and then three miles to his own house, where his mother and sisters were in the garden some distance away. They acted on their son's warning and the next morning at daylight the Indians attacked and ransacked their home, destroying whatever they couldn't carry off. At the same time, the family made it safely to the Bartlett ranch.

The previous evening when the Shanahans didn't show up, 'Yank' told his son to pull his boots off and crawl out without making any noise, then get to Oro Blanco and tell the people what had happened, especially to send someone to his partner 'Hank' Hewitt's place and to fetch Dr. Noon to come and see Shanahan. Johnny slipped out about 8 o'clock and carried his boots two miles, then put them on and raced off until he came to a ranch five miles from Oro Blanco. He got there at midnight and woke up three men who had returned earlier to find the Indians had pillaged the place and made off with guns, ammunition, clothing, and drained a bottle of brandy. Johnny and one of the men headed on to Oro Blanco and by two A.M. told the people there all about "the trouble over at our house," as he put it when telling his story later.

Fourteen people from Oro Blanco and thereabouts quickly fitted themselves out with horses, saddles and arms, and rode back to Bear Valley. Johnny wanted to go too, but his mother firmly forbade it. When the relief party got to the Bartlett ranch they found Shanahan mortally wounded, 'Yank' slightly so, and the Indians gone. 'Yank' and 'Hank' had been partners in raising fine blooded mares and colts, but the raiders drove off forty to sixty of these animals.

Shanahan died the last day of April, leaving a widow and four children, for whom the people of Oro Blanco raised a purse of $50. The Army arrived too late to be of any help and, after skirmishing in the days to come, the Apaches faded back into Mexico. Four months later, Geronimo and his followers finally surrendered at Skeleton Canyon in the southeastern corner of Arizona.

The names Yank Canyon and Yank's Spring together with a Forest Service plaque today mark the Indian raids in Bear Valley and the desperate runs by two ten-year-old boys to rescue their families.

REFERENCES

Arizona Daily Star (Tucson), May 2, 4, 6, 11, 20, 23, 1886.
Wilbur-Cruce, Eva Antonia. *A Beautiful, Cruel Country.* Tucson: University of Arizona Press, 1987.
Willson, Roscoe G. "A ten-year-old boy is hero at Geronimo raid." *Arizona Days & Ways*, July 1, 1956, pp. 30-31.
Willson, Roscoe G. "Geronimo foiled by a boy." *Arizona* (supplement to *The Arizona Republic*), May 18, 1975, pp. 56-57.

12

Farming for Feathers

If it had been called "ranching," there would be shelves of books about it. But because it was considered *farming*, the once-prized raising of ostriches in Arizona is now nearly forgotten. From the 1890s through the early twentieth century, farmers in the Salt River Valley saw rosy prospects in raising ostriches to sell their highly-valued plumage.

Ostrich plumes had adorned rulers and the well-to-do since ancient times, but until the nineteenth century all ostrich feathers supplied to Europe were obtained from wild birds, hunted and killed in North Africa and Arabia. The business of raising ostriches commercially for their feathers began in South Africa, when an eclectic mixture of immigrants—Lithuanian Jews (fleeing from pograms), Africaaners, Englishmen, and Scots turned a scrubby, semi-desert landscape known as the Little Karoo into a giant ostrich ranch, centered around the town of Oudtshoorn in Western Cape Province. Within a decade or two many of the farmers there metamorphosed into wealthy ostrich barons by catering to the demands of fashion for the elegant plumes of these birds. The feather boas, opera cloaks and outsized hats of stylish ladies included the wing and tail feathers from ostriches of both sexes. An average hat might require three big wing feathers, two good tail feathers, and some "odds and ends." The prices for plumes soared in value to become, ounce for ounce, more precious than gold. The boom stretched from the 1880s to 1914.

The South African feather merchants who supplied the needs of fashion swelled the domesticated ostrich population to one million birds by 1913 and built themselves feather palaces from the proceeds—huge mansions of ochre-colored sandstone that one writer characterized as "mixing the wildest excesses of Ottoman, Victorian, Greek and Gothic architecture."[1] All of this in little more than a generation.

Ostriches were native to South Africa and many other parts of the continent. Farmers at Oudtshoorn had domesticated the native blue-necked subspecies in the 1850s. With the arrival of alfalfa, it was soon learned that ostriches thrived on it, and raising the birds for their plumes paid far better than any other form of agriculture. The flightless avions were placed in large fenced areas and soon began to multiply, the number of breeding birds rising to well over 20,000 by 1875. Between 1875 and 1880, the new livestock was selling for up to £1,000 a pair. The minimal amount of capital needed led to the emergence of many new ostrich farmers.[2]

South Africans at Oudtshoorn continued as the principal suppliers and took notice when their birds, which were actually hybrids, began to produce plumes that were less than perfect. They needed flocks that would blow away any competition, especially the Americans. So the South African government sponsored what became the Great Trans-Saharan Ostrich Expedition to find more of a legendary variety of these birds called Barbaries. The crossing of four of these with the native birds in the 1870s had produced black-necked offspring, with unimaginably opulent plumes, giving the Oudtshoorn farmers their supremacy in the market. The expeditionaries had little to go on when they took ship to West Africa, then proceeded 500 miles up the Niger River to continue on their journey by railroad until the rail line ran out at the lip of the Sahara. Their search led them hundreds of miles to the west in an incredible saga that involved dodging French legionnaires as they penetrated into what was then French West Africa, until they finally found an emir with 156 of the magnificent birds. They bought all of these. The adventure continued until 134 of the Barbaries were toted and shipped back to Cape Town, where they arrived on May 25, 1912, ten months after the expedition began. Time unfortunately was not on their side; two years later the market for plumes collapsed.[3]

Although buyers for ostrich plumes vanished with the start of World War I in 1914, the industry continued on a much more modest scale and the number of birds around Oudtshoorn today is estimated at 200,000 to 300,000. This city, slightly smaller than Yuma, Arizona, remains the worldwide center of ostrich farming.[4]

The introduction of ostriches to the United States probably followed from a consular report, "Ostrich Farming in the United States," issued by the Department of State in October 1882. In this, U.S. consuls Baker of Buenos Ayres (where ostriches had recently been introduced) and Siler in Cape Town, South Africa, reported in detail on ostrich raising in their areas and stressed the extremely favorable economic returns that could be anticipated.[5] In 1885

Edwin Cawston of South Pasadena, California, took note and chartered a ship to bring fifty of "the best obtainable ostriches in the world" from South Africa to Galveston, Texas, whence the birds endured a train journey to California. Of the original fifty, only eighteen survived, and they became the basis for the Cawston Ostrich Farm that opened in 1886.[6] However, another source claims that ostriches arrived in southern California two years earlier.

Whichever is right, ostriches first came to Arizona in 1892, when about twenty birds were brought into the territory from California. The climate in Arizona proved to be ideal, and around 1906 the raising of these exotic creatures expanded rapidly until by 1911 the Phoenix area and the Salt River Valley reportedly had more than 6,000 head. The stock of the largest raiser, the Pan-American Ostrich Company, numbered at least 2,000 birds. There were other large farms and even individual farmers kept from two to ten of the fowls.

Newspapers carried detailed reports on this new industry. Plumes were the principal product, and an elaborate terminology for these came into use. A lesser market existed for the chicks and eggs. No one suggested roasting or eating an ostrich, and the use of their skins as leather was rarely mentioned.

Agricultural writers stressed the economics of raising ostriches as compared with cattle. An ostrich might live to the age of eighty and produce plumage for fifty years. A bird was plucked (the feathers were actually cut) every eight months for a total of about $45 in feathers per year—the same value as a three-year-old steer. An ostrich of this age would be worth from $200 to $250, and especially fine breeding birds brought much more.[7] A visitor to an ostrich farm near Phoenix in 1908 wrote back to Indiana, "Was Out to the Ostrich Farm Saturday. Seen a plume worth thirty-eight dollars. How many do you want."[8]

Any creature that weighed 300 to 400 pounds at maturity and had a brain the size of a golf ball was probably not the brightest animal in the farmyard, but it did have a sort of aggressive curiosity. One writer claimed "The ostrich is a very serious bird" and that "the ostrich's stomach is like the hog's." He might better have said that they ate anything that came their way, as anyone who entered an enclosure risked having buttons, jewelry, and every bright object picked off their clothing and gulped down. An ostrich would eat anything it could swallow, including the staples, nails and wire ends left by fencing crews.

Every ostrich's dream food was fresh, chopped alfalfa, six to eight pounds of it each day, although growers today apparently depend upon a blend of soybean meal, corn, and other prepared feed. On one occasion, a big male bird in Arizona followed his instincts:

"The voraciousness of the ostrich is proverbial; and at the Pickrell farm one of the big males got into a ludicrous situation because of this. Within the enclosure where this bird was is a corn crib, filled with corn on the ear. One day the small door was left open by an employee, and soon the ostrich discovered it. By much maneuvering he managed to get into the crib and began to gorge. 'A belly full' was insufficient, and he ate on till his neck was full to the very bill. He ate it cob and all, the cobs going down lengthwise. So, when he wanted to leave the crib and enjoy digesting the meal, he couldn't bend his neck to get out the door. He tried in every possible way, but the neck full of corncobs wouldn't bend, and he stormed about the crib quite furiously till the men were compelled to knock out a lot of the slats of which the crib was made and permit him to emerge."[9]

University of Arizona researchers turned their attention to the world's largest bird only in 1915. The fourteen birds that made up the University's flock occupied part of the school's new five-acre poultry farm. Robert H. Forbes, the Dean of Agriculture, proved a friend of the flock, and the Agricultural Experiment Station's annual report for 1915 included a section on its ostrich investigations. But fashions had changed, and by the beginning of World War I the Gibson Girl was no more and the demand for ostrich plumes had plummeted, along with hopes for a continuation of the industry. The daughters of Edwardian ladies became the flappers of the 1920s. Only in 1986 did interest revive, and since 1989 Chandler, Arizona, has proudly sponsored an annual Ostrich Festival. The Rooster Cogburn Ostrich Ranch welcomes visitors at Picacho Peak, but commercial ostrich-raising in the United States has diminished to a might-have-been.

Ostrich farm near Phoenix, 1908. (Postcard courtesy of the author)

Plucking ostrich plumes, c. 1908.
(Postcard courtesy of the author)

Message on card: 'They sure can go some', c. 1926. (Postcard courtesy of the author)

Feather Palace at Oudtshoorn, 1910. (Courtesy of Welgeluk Feather Palace)

Notes

1. Nixon, Rob. *Dreambirds*, p. 5. New York: Picador USA, 2000.
2. "Oudtshoorn, Ostrich Capital of the World." Online at www.seligman.org.il/oudtshoorn_history.html.
3. Nixon, *Dreambirds*, pp. 78-88.
4. Shanawany, M.M., and John Dingle. "Ostrich production systems." United Nations Food and Agriculture Organization, FAO Animal Production and Health Paper 144 (1999), p. 168. Online at www.fao.org/3/a-x2370e.pdf.
5. Online at this title.
6. Online at books.google.com/ostriches/cawston.
7. Dinsmore, Chas. A. "On Ostrich Farm," *Arizona Daily Star*, September 10, 1911, Second Section, p. 3. *Reports of the Department of the Interior for the Fiscal Year Ended June 30, 1909*, p. 542, Admininstrative Reports, Vol. II. Washington: Government Printing Office, 1910.
8. Postcard in the author's collection.
9. Dinsmore, op. cit.

An earlier version of this chapter appeared in the April 2003 issue of *Arizona Senior World*.

13

THE HOUSE BY THE SIDE OF THE ROAD

Between Springerville and St. Johns in east-central Arizona, a road leads east from highway US 666 towards the Springerville Generating Station. The road crosses the Little Colorado River Valley at a point known as the Richville Valley, perhaps named for the Richey family, whose members lived there as early as the 1880s.[1] About 1 km. beyond the river lie the ruins of a small stone house, site AZ Q:11:66 in the Arizona State Museum numbering system, just outside the north right-of-way fence.

The house is apparently well-known to local residents, but not so the story behind it. This chapter is a history of that dwelling—who built it, when, why, and who lived there. The findings also help to illustrate the use of little-known records for the history of homesteading.[2]

This structure posed a question when it was first recorded as a historic site in 1978, in that it lay upon State of Arizona lands, specifically in the NW¼ of the SE¼ of Section 2, Township 10 North, Range 28 East, Apache County, Arizona. This parcel is part of what is called a school section and came to the State from the Federal government as a result of the 1910 Enabling Act.[3] The mystery was, why would anyone build a house on land that they did not own?

The House

The little stone house is located downslope from the road on a small pediment surface. This surface is heavily dissected by arroyos that have been there for at least ninety years. Construction of the present road eliminated most of the ridge line that once rose immediately to the southeast of the house site. The situation is a peculiar one in that the dwelling was not convenient to farmlands or to the Little Colorado River valley, and a wagon or automobile could not have reached it directly at the time of its construction. There was evidently no water supply closer than the river and the ridge line lay on the wrong side to offer any protection from prevailing storms.

The building's walls are roughly shaped blocks and slabs of locally available sandstone, two courses in width, laid up by a skilled mason using adobe mortar. The walls have no separate foundations. Large quoins bond the corners. Sections of the walls still stand up to 2.8 meters in height. The structure is square, the sides each 8.44 meters in length with the corners at the cardinal points of the compass. Doorways in the northeast and southwest walls are positioned off-center towards the northwest. The door frames still lie upon the surface nearby. The manner in which the northwest and southeast walls are tumbling suggests that each wall had two casement windows. The only indications of a roof are two small pieces of corrugated sheet iron among the debris. Inside the house are scraps of lumber and fallen masonry, but no evidence for interior partitions. Scattered on the surface outside are a few artifacts from daily living—pieces of bottle glass, ceramics, and metal. Violet-colored container glass suggests an age of early twentieth century.

Architecturally this house belongs to a class of square, hip-roofed dwellings associated especially with homesteaders and company-built housing during the early twentieth century. The best surviving example of this style nearby is the Voigt ranch house, about 3 km. from the Springerville Generating Station. The Voigt ranch began as a homestead built in the fall of 1916 and is still used on Mr. Harold LeSueur's ranch.[4]

The Records

Because the school section belongs to the State of Arizona, the land has not been privately owned and there would be no abstract or chain of title. This left a possibility that the house might have been part of an unsuccessful homestead claim.

From 1812 until 1946, the U.S. General Land Office (GLO) administered the public land laws of the United States. After 1862, an increasing amount of the agency's work involved individual settlement claims on public lands under a series of homesteading laws. These laws established eligibility requirements for claimants, known as entrymen, and the conditions under which they could acquire tracts from the public domain. The process began with an initial filing, called an entry, after which an entryman normally had three to five years to meet the government's conditions concerning residence on the land and cultivation of it. To meet these requirements was termed proving-up.

The proving-up period on a claim saw a series of filings that accumulated in a homestead case file, identified by the name of the applicant and a serial number. A homesteader's house, cultivated lands and other improvements will be listed here, often with additional details about family history and economic activities. Case files normally contain quite a full account of the manner in which homesteaded lands passed from the public domain into private ownership. Eventually there were many ways, here called entry systems, by which an entryman could prove-up on a claim and receive a patent or title to it.

The early twentieth century was the peak period of homesteading. The dozen or so years after 1909 saw so many new homesteading laws enacted that a person could practically custom-tailor an entry system to suit his or her individual situation. This was all quite legal and potential entrymen, lawyers, and GLO personnel knew how these laws and their accompanying regulations worked. Such knowledge is now obsolete and the GLO itself was abolished in 1946 when its functions were transferred to the newly-created Bureau of Land Management (BLM).

Voluminous homesteading records are housed today at the National Archives and Records Administration in Washington, DC and at the regional branches of the National Archives. To locate the records for a particular homestead claim, one begins with the serial number assigned at the time of the initial filing. This number can normally be found on a serial register card at the BLM state office. The serial number in turn will lead to a homestead case file.

Files exist for unsuccessful claims as well as for the ones that were patented. Assuming that a researcher finds a serial number or numbers for these unpatented claims, there are two types of case files, both now located at the National Archives. The serial files of cancelled entries are administered by that agency. The unpatented serial applications are still in the legal custody of the BLM. Access is granted to both types of records, but getting to the desired files is a complex process. In some cases, details found on serial register cards at the state BLM office and in unpatented files may be even more voluminous than those for the successful claims.

The serial register card for the SW¼ of Section 1 in the same township included the northern half of the SE¼ of Section 2 as well. This card led directly to Thomas R. Irwin's unpatented Serial Application File 029697. The BLM in Washington returned this file to their Arizona State Office, where a copy was made available to me. The file was full of information about Irwin himself and the progress of his claim, but a question remained as to whether it applied as well to the small stone house in Section 2. This question was finally resolved in

October 1987 when I interviewed Mr. Celso Madrid of Eager, Arizona. As a young boy he had lived in the house. Unless otherwise referenced, the following reconstruction of events is based upon the applications and other records in Thomas Irwin's unpatented Serial Application File.

In the Beginning: Thomas R. Irwin

Thomas R. Irwin, or Uncle Tom Irwin as one informant called him, was a Canadian by birth and naturalized as a United States citizen on May 7, 1895, in Coconino County, Arizona. His early history is not known. He was married and had a family, including at least one son. In 1901 he filed a homestead claim on the Black Mesa Forest Reserve for a 160-acre tract located about five miles northeast of Greer, Arizona. He built a three-room log house, barn granary, corral and stable, placed some five acres under cultivation, and lived there for about three years. Irwin also had a sawmill on this claim, but "a government man" ordered him to stop cutting timber. He removed the sawmill, then found that he could not make a living and so moved away in September of 1910. A letter of April 14, 1911, notified him that his claim was cancelled.

Sometime prior to 1918 and probably before 1916, Tom Irwin purchased or leased a farm in the Richville Valley just north of where the road from US 666 now crosses the valley. The Irwins lived in a house known as "the Mexican House" situated near a spring directly below the malpais on the west side of the Little Colorado.[5] It was during this period that Thomas Irwin filed what was called a second entry. This was a homestead claim on the land initially included in his Serial Application No. 029697. Documents accumulated in this case file for twenty years.

Thomas Irwin's Homestead Claim

Irwin's second entry was a misadventure almost from its beginning. His application was dated March 3, 1916, under the Acts of February 19, 1909, and September 5, 1914. The 1909 Act was called the Enlarged Homestead Law. It permitted a claim up to 320 acres in size, of land not susceptible to irrigation, and required that the claimant reside on the land and continuously cultivate part of it for at least three years. The 1914 law allowed entries under the public land laws by persons who had lost, forfeited or abandoned an earlier claim through no fault of their own.[6] As of March 9th, Thomas Irwin made application for tracts in Section 1, Section 2, and Section 11, totaling 320 acres, all in Township

10 North, Range 28 East. What he should have done at this point was to hire a lawyer to clarify the status of these lands.

His application was immediately suspended until the GLO could designate these lands as being subject to entry under the Enlarged Homestead Act. On March 16, 1916, Irwin filed a petition asking that the lands be so designated. His initial filing was now completed. For the next two years, Tom Irwin heard nothing about the status of his claim. The silence was not unusual. Whether Irwin genuinely thought that he could fulfill the homesteading requirements is not known. He probably hoped to use the homestead to 'block-up' the land holdings that he already held on either side of his second entry. This, of course, was not a goal of the homesteading laws.

On April 1, 1918, Irwin inquired directly of the Secretary of the Interior about his homestead entry, specifically to ask about taking a leave of absence. A reply dated April 23 advised him that the lands applied for had not yet been designated as subject to entry. Significantly, Tom Irwin was also told that "Any residence, cultivation, or improvements had by you on the lands applied for prior to the allowance of your application would be had at your own risk should your application not be allowed."

Actually, there was some confusion, since the Secretary of the Interior *had* included the lands in Irwin's application in a designation approved on March 15, 1918, to be effective as of May 10. In May, the GLO wrote to both Thomas Irwin and to the Register and Receiver of the U.S. Land Office in Phoenix, Arizona, saying that Irwin's application was approved in the absence of any objection. The Register and Receiver promptly notified Washington that Section 2 was State school land and the application should have been rejected when it was filed! Section 2 had passed to the State under the grant for the use of schools, made by the Enabling Act of June 20, 1910. Irwin did not learn of this development until after April 30, 1919, when the GLO in Washington formally disallowed his application.

The GLO allowed Tom Irwin to file an amended application. He did so in May 1919, applying now for 320 acres in Section 1 of the same township. Five years later the designation of this tract received approval, but Irwin may no longer have been living in the area. He vacated the Richville Valley before 1923, and by 1927 he had found employment as a locomotive engineer at Victorville, California. Irwin, still at Victorville, finally relinquished his amended entry in 1936.

Thomas Irwin's Stone House: AZ Q:11:66

The GLO letter of April 23, 1918, advising that "Any residence...would be had at your own risk...," turned out to be prophetic. After completing his initial filing back in 1916, Irwin had been quite industrious. When he wrote to the Secretary of the Interior two years later, he mentioned, "I have a house built of stone all finished but part of the wood work & I had the lumber paid for but the mill burned down. Tom Danley told me he would rebuild it this spring. I had a small frame shack on it but I tore it down to help build the other place."

Much later, Irwin swore that he had lived on the land for six months from October 1916 until April 1917 and that he erected a house on what he thought was a part of the premises. In another affidavit he explained, "I have built a house which I presumed was on the land but after a survey was made I found that the house was not built on this land."

Since this activity all transpired between the date of his initial filing and the GLO rejection of his application in 1919, the house must have been built on the lands *not* approved for designation, i.e., in Sections 2 or 11. So far as is known, the ruins at AZ Q:11:66 are the only remains of a stone house situated on or adjacent to the lands claimed in the initial filing of Irwin's second entry. As he confessed later, "he erected a house on what he thought was a part of the said premises but...it later proved to be on other lands."

Mr. Celso Madrid of Eager, Arizona, 78 years old as of 1987, recalled that as a small boy he had lived in this stone house with his foster parents, Mr. and Mrs. Robert Madrid. He thought that they moved there in or about 1917 and stayed for around two years—during the period of the influenza epidemic after World War I. Robert Madrid worked for Thomas Irwin at this time, farming on the west side of the Little Colorado in the Richville Valley.

Celso Madrid also recalled a number of specific details about the house. He did not know who had built it or whether anyone had occupied the dwelling before or after the Madrids lived there. The house was divided down the middle at the time by a partition of 2 x 4 timbers. Mr. Madrid thought that Thomas Irwin might have put in this dividing wall. The Madrids lived only in the northern (actually northwestern) section. This part was covered by a shed roof made of corrugated iron, the downslope of the roof being towards the northwest. It was a cold place in the winter, a fireplace in the west corner furnishing the only heat. The southern half of the house stood completely open.

The coincidence between Celso Madrid's statements as to the time when he and his family lived in the stone house, his foster father's employment by

Tom Irwin, and the obviously unfinished state of the building confirm that this is the structure described in the unpatented serial application file. When Irwin petitioned in March of 1916 for the lands in Section 2 to be declared open to entry, the GLO should have disallowed his claim immediately because that section was already owned by the State of Arizona.

However, Thomas Irwin proceeded to fence the land, dig a well, and between October 1916 and April 1917, build a stone house upon it. Under the conditions of the Enlarged Homestead Act, he was required to maintain continuous residence for three years, cultivate a minimum of twenty acres during the second year, and forty acres during the third year. He may have done none of these; instead, Robert Madrid and his family occupied the house for upwards of two years, 1917–1919.

Then on April 1, 1918, Tom Irwin asked the Secretary of the Interior for permission to take a leave of absence "on my filing" because of a local drought. He mentioned his improvements including the house but did not say that he was living in it. The GLO denied this request because the lands had not even been designated as subject to entry. Several weeks later, the U.S. Land Office in Phoenix discovered that Section 2 was State land. They notified the GLO in Washington, but no one told Irwin of this discovery. He received the bad news a year later, in the April 30, 1919 letter.

Tom Irwin had built his house in the wrong place—on a State school section. The mistake should have been caught at the time of his initial filing, but it was not. Three years passed before he received formal notice that the part of his claim with the house on it was not available for entry. The Madrid family may have been the only persons to live in this dwelling. At some later time, the wood in it was salvaged except for two door frames. Since then the structure has weathered naturally, with little or no obvious vandalism. As of 1987 the house that Tom Irwin should have built somewhere else lies just outside the right-of-way of a heavily travelled access road. Hopefully the walls will still be standing many years from now.

Acknowledgments: At various times from 1978 through 1987 I talked with the following persons about this house: Milburn and Gloria Sherwood of the Richville Valley; Jeff Hammond of St. Johns, Arizona, and Messrs. Larry Sherwood and Celso Madrid of Springerville and Eager, Arizona. The cooperation of the BLM offices in both Phoenix and Washington DC is also much appreciated. An earlier version of this chapter appeared in *The Kiva*, Vol. 53/4 (1988).

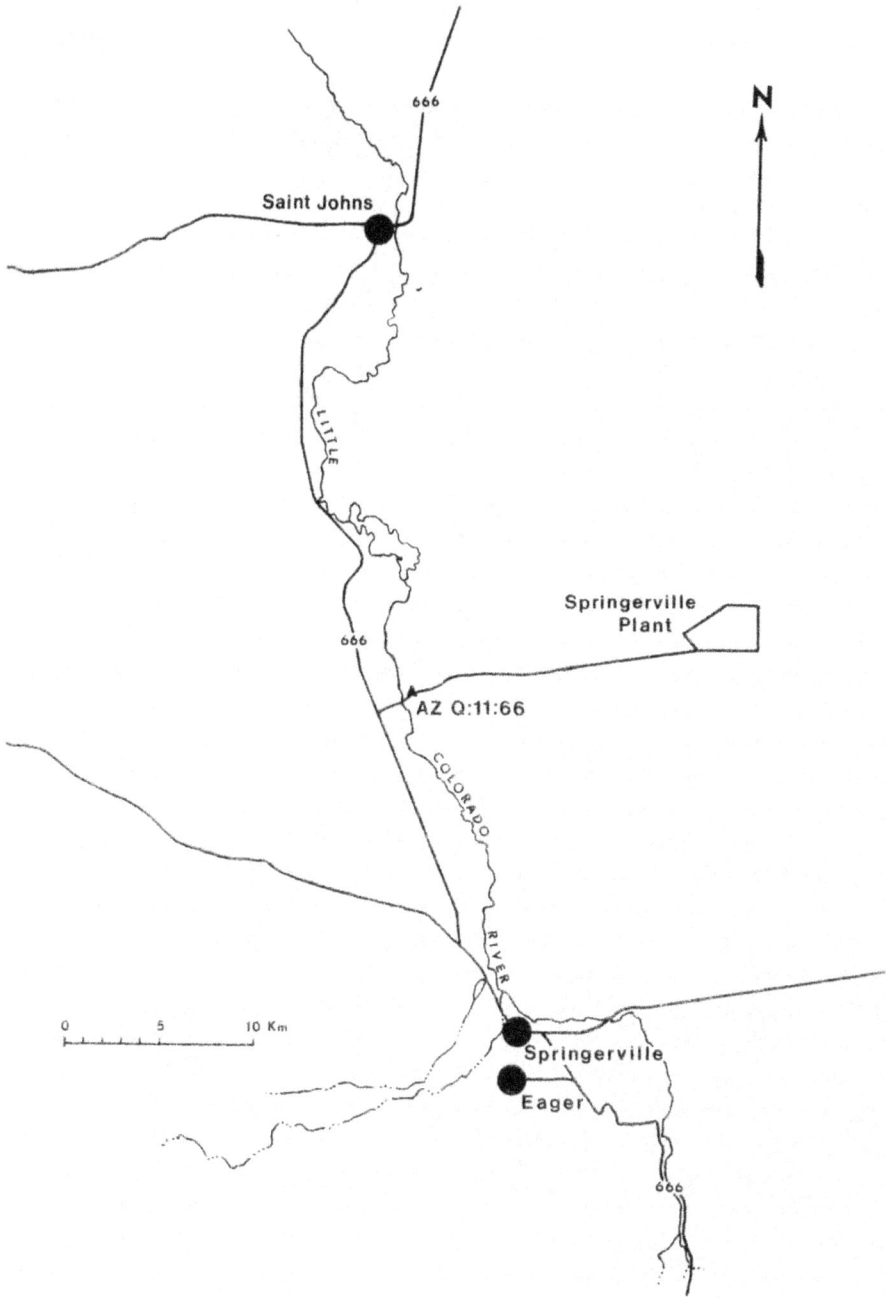

Richville valley, Arizona. (Map courtesy of the author)

Southeast and southwest sides of the Bob Madrid house.
(Photograph courtesy of the author, 1982)

South corner of the Bob Madrid house.
(Photograph courtesy of the author, 1982)

Voigt (LeSueur) ranch house, built in 1916. (Photograph courtesy of the author, 1980)

NOTES

1. Charles A. Hoffman, A Survey of Historic Sites in the Little Colorado Valley, Arizona. In *Forgotten Places and Things: Archaeological Perspectives on American History*, edited by Albert E. Ward, p. 113. Center for Anthropological Studies, Albuquerque, 1983. C. LeRoy and Mable R. Wilhelm, *A History of the St. Johns Stake,* pp. 72, 266. Historical Publications, Orem, Utah, 1982.
2. John P. Wilson, *The El Paso Electric Survey, Amrad to Eddy County, Southeastern New Mexico*. Report on file at the Arizona State Museum Library, University of Arizona, Tucson, 1984.
3. Thomas R. Irwin, Unpatented Serial Application File, Phoenix #029697, for Thomas R. Irwin, 1916-1936, on file at Washington Records Center. Available through U.S. Department of the Interior, Bureau of Land Management, Office of Information Assistance, Branch of Records. Washington, DC.
4. John P. Wilson, *Archeological Surveys of Proposed Material Pits and Well-Monitoring Facilities Associated With the Springerville Generating Station, Apache County, Arizona, Appendix I*. Report on file at the Arizona State Museum Library, University of Arizona, Tucson, 1980.
5. Hoffman 1983: 112-113; Milburn Sherwood, personal communication, June 18, 1978.
6. U.S. Department of the Interior, General Land Office, *Suggestions to Homesteaders and Persons Desiring to Make Homestead Entries. Circular No. 541*, pp. 34, 39-41. U.S. Government Printing Office, Washington, DC, 1926.

I4

BLACK GOLD IN THE SAN SIMON

Arizona is an oil-producing state? It became one in 1955, when the first well came in. From a high point of almost 3,000,000 barrels in 1967, twenty-five wells in three small fields near Lukachukai, in the far northeastern corner of our state, yielded a total of just 60,072 barrels of oil in 2013. This dropped to about 13,000 barrels in 2017 with no significant production since then. Two of the early fields, Dry Mesa and Teec Nos Pos, produced 830,000 and 486,000 barrels respectively before being plugged or abandoned in the 1990s. The largest oil field has been Dineh-bi-Kayah, "The People's Field," which pumped a total of 18,703,386 barrels of oil from January 1967 to January 1, 2013. Altogether since 1954, Arizona wells have been the source of more than 21 million barrels of the liquid gold.[1]

The completion of commercial oil wells was preceded by more than fifty years of searching, much of this in southeastern Arizona, where showings of oil invariably turned into dry holes. Exploration was spurred initially by discoveries in surrounding states, beginning with southern California in the 1890s and then the Spindletop oil field near Beaumont, Texas, in 1901. An Arizona newspaper in 1897 reported that a person in St. David had struck a stratum that yielded a "dark yellowish color" of oil at 200 feet while drilling for artesian water.[2] Nothing came of this.

The first recorded well test in Arizona was completed in 1903, and from that time until the first commercial oil well was brought in 1955, about 164 wells are known to have been drilled.[3] The object of some of these was to find water; how many sought oil or natural gas is not known. The U.S. Geological Survey tabulated four wells completed there between 1905 and 1910, four more through 1919, another six before 1927, and twenty-two between 1927 and 1931.[4] Southeastern Arizona witnessed some of this activity.

Primary source materials about this aspect of Arizona's history lie in the records of the Arizona Geological Survey, the Arizona Corporation Commission, and newspapers of the period. These show that oil drilling began as ventures of small companies organized in Arizona to search for and produce oil, carried on by persons who had no previous experience in the business. Wildcatters, in other words.

The records of individual wells at the Arizona Geological Survey and contemporary newspaper accounts allow us to reconstruct the ups and downs of the early drilling ventures, especially the oil "boom" in the San Simon Valley between 1927 and 1931. By 1927, more than a dozen test wells had already been drilled. One early article reported that Perry Howie's well north of Bowie, Arizona, found "showings" of oil and gas in the summer of 1912, but then one night, "After myself and another had gone to bed, the well blew in, throwing oil and gas over the derrick, and did so for nine days and nights, and eventually ruined the hole and sealed itself off. No effort was made to reopen the well."[5]

One summary of wildcatting efforts mentioned the U.S. Oil Co. No.1 well, completed in 1917:

> "One of the first holes to be drilled was the U.S. well located north of Bowie about ten miles. They went down better than 1000 feet. They seemed to have had plenty of oil showings but eventually they quit work, pulled their casing and departed."[6]

A visit to this well site in 1996 showed plenty of evidence of an oil-drilling operation, but no trace of casing that would indicate the actual drilling location. Late in 1927, one of the boilers at the steam engine for a well being drilled near Pima, Arizona exploded and scattered parts of the rig across the countryside. One worker received burns.[7]

The five years from 1927 through 1931 witnessed a peak in drilling activity, amounting to a boom in oil exploration. Twenty-two wells were completed and the Bowie newspaper even renamed itself the San Simon Valley Oil News. Recent oil discoveries in California and New Mexico apparently started this, and Arizona businessmen sought the opinions of geologists. In the northwestern corner of New Mexico drillers had employed conventional wisdom and located, with good results, on anticlines or domes where crude oil had accumulated in traps. In Arizona the geologists made similar recommendations, although some test holes may have been drilled on the strength of oil and gas showings in water wells.[8]

In the San Simon Valley, geologists were optimistic, although the actual choice of drilling sites seems to have depended on several types of "oil-detecting instruments." Arizona newspapers of the 1927-28 period made a number of references to at least three types of instruments. One of these, the Trumbull Seismograph, satisfied geologist Claude Palmer that "the instrument had an affinity to petroliferous content."[9] The operators hastened to assure everyone that this and other devices were not "doodle-bug contraptions," in the language of the times. The only account in the literature of how any of these worked was given by one Wm. J. Vaughan, cited as the local manager of the Underwriters' Syndicate and superintendent of the well being drilled on a lease at Pima, Arizona:

> "There are two types of detectors. One reacts to the presence of oil and indicates volume. The other indicates only the depth at which oil may be struck. The first type may be described as an affinity instrument. It carries a reservoir of compound chemicals similar to those contained in petroleum. These chemicals are sympathetic to the vibrations sent out by electrons of the petroleum atoms and respond when the reservoir is suspended over a subterranean reservoir of oil. Amplifiers similar to those used in magnifying radio vibrations step up the sympathetic vibrations in the container until they can be mechanically indicated on a dial."[10]

To the tekkies of the late 1920s this may all have been very clear. To others, it probably smacked of water-witching; i.e., if you find what you're looking for, it works; if not, find another place to try it.

The oil ventures in Arizona began as locally-based operations, although some were bought out later by interests from Utah, California and New York. Always short of capital, rarely did a company drill more than a single well at a time, or more than three altogether. The large display ads to encourage oil speculation that are found in newspapers elsewhere, as with an oil "boom" in the Tularosa Basin of southern New Mexico in 1919–1920, are missing in Arizona. As late as 1931 the Pinal Oil Co. claimed that it "is fully financed and...all negotiations for purchase of that company's stock are cancelled."[11] The Arizona drillers had an honest intention of finding oil.

The stories of two wildcatters' holes, about fourteen miles north of Bowie, are typical of this search activity in the San Simon Valley. Articles of incorporation for the Whitlock Oil Company were filed September 8, 1926 with Temple F. Penrod of Phoenix, described as a "well known auto accessory salesman" as the president, and Bob Thomas, then of Globe, Arizona, as statutory agent. One of the incorporators, Boyd Lind of Yuma, Arizona, evidently was the inventor of the Lind oil-detecting instrument. The company did not issue stock and instead spent time until the following April in raising capital. According to their only Annual Report on file, Whitlock held an oil and gas lease on Section 36, T10S R28E, on State of Arizona lands, which became the location of their Prospect No. 1.

The entrepreneurs drilled their own well instead of using a subcontractor, which would have been unusual for the day, especially for an organization with no prior experience in the field. One photograph of their well, the Whitlock No. 1, shows a crew of five men plus a young girl, probably the cook.[12] Drilling finally began on July 3, 1927, and was done entirely with a cable-tool drilling rig. Whether this was powered by a steam or a gasoline engine is not known for certain, but an early progress report said that the well had struck water at 150 feet and drilling was suspended until completion of a water well nearby. This implies the possible use of a steam engine. However, two articles from 1931 mentioned one or more gasoline engines at the Whitlock Oil Co. Well No. 1. A 1927 photograph showed a simplified drill rig with a small derrick, a single roofed shelter and four small cabins. The undated later photograph shown here indicates a more elaborate derrick guyed up by cables, surrounded by a camp. The rigs in the two views are not the same equipment.

By the end of August the well had been drilled below 1,200 feet, at which point a series of shut-downs began while the drillers either waited for the arrival of new casing or were occupied with a series of attempts to shut-off underground water flows. Finally, on December 4, the Phoenix and Globe newspapers carried major stories on the discovery of oil in Arizona. The Whitlock well had come in on November 9th below 1,400 feet with a production estimated at 1,000 to 7,000 barrels of oil per day. In the month before this announcement, the company had been buying up other leases. After the December announcement, reporting on this well virtually ceased in the local newspapers, apart from allusions to attempts to secure a water shutoff.[13] Mr. Penrod added that arrangements had been made with Los Angeles banks to finance the Whitlock Co. "until arrangements for delivery of the oil are completed." The owners had evidently expended their capital and were now reduced to borrowing outside of their original ring of resources.

Although the level with the oil sand had been plugged for the time being, a careful reader would see that a serious problem with water existed. The water was hot, with a temperature of more than 100° F. and a discharge estimated at

500,000 gallons per day, flowing under artesian conditions. Initial attempts to control it, as reported in *The Arizona Republican*, may seem naïve:

> "Oil has been flowing with the water over both slush pits at the well and through the ditches as far as three quarters of a mile across the desert. A vast earthen dam has been constructed at some distance from the well, and as soon as the cementing off process is completed, oil will be permitted to flow out into this huge reservoir until tank or pipe line construction can be completed, Mr. Penrod said."[14]

This reservoir may yet be seen on the USGS Javelina Peak 7.5' topo map. Company officials "freely predicted" that "Whitlock No. 1 had written the first line of a new chapter in Arizona's history." Unwarranted optimism flowed more freely than oil, and while the underground flows were apparently brought under some control, drillers were not able to effect a water shut-off, which effectively doomed any further development. A well log at the Arizona Geological Survey, USGS records, and later newspaper reports differ as to the eventual depth of the well and the depths at which the oil sand and water flows were encountered. The company was reorganized in the spring of 1929 and its proprietors moved on.

Drilling equipment remained in place there as recently as 1931. Today, two large pieces of the drilling rig lie alongside the road in to the old Whitlock No. 1 well location. The land became Federal property through an exchange with the State of Arizona in 1989, and the Arizona Bureau of Land Management has developed this as its Hot Well Dunes Recreation Area. Hot water still flows from the original well, but it is now channeled into two hot tubs and a wading pool before it runs off across the desert.

A short distance north of this site lies the original well head for the Bear Springs Oil & Gas Co. Pinal 1 well, drilled by the Pinal Oil Co. The story of this well parallels that of the first one, but involves two companies; the Bear Springs Oil & Gas Company (exploration) and the Pinal Oil Co. (drilling). The former was incorporated on April 3, 1926 to drill for, produce and deal in oil, and to engage in business. Two of its officers were also officers in the Whitlock Oil Co. Bob Thomas was the statutory agent. This company had few assets and little capital at any time, and while the assets had decreased to $2.08 in 1931, the amount of paid-up stock increased to almost $12,500 that same year.[15]

The historical background of the Pinal Oil Co. is both more complex and confusing. It was organized specifically to drill for oil and gas, acquire leases and build pipelines. The incorporators, directors and officers were largely the same persons in the two years following its incorporation on February 3, 1927. The company prospered initially, at least on paper, and sometime between the summer of 1928 and February 1929 a completely new set of officers assumed control. The organization apparently engaged in very little drilling activity and the record of shares authorized, splits and new shares authorized hint that business activities may have lain mostly with stock speculations. The *San Simon Valley Oil News* for November 2, 1928, carried an informative profile of the Pinal Oil Co. So far as can be determined, this company drilled only one well.[16]

The drilling crew spudded in the Bear Springs Oil & Gas Co. Pinal 1 well sometime in early March, 1927. By mid-month they had penetrated to 300 feet, and three weeks later to 500 feet. The first big news was that gas pressure had forced quicksand almost to the top of the hole, and "big oil showings have been obtained by bailers" while "the slush pit is said to be covered with oil." The driller, William Crawford, was faced with drilling and casing a new well.[17] Both the initial Keystone rig and its replacement, an old No. 7 Star rig, were evidently steam-powered. Progress was slow until August 17, when a tornado demolished the derrick and blew over the bunk houses. Three weeks later a new derrick and the replacement cable-tool machinery were in place. The crew "plugged along steadily" until mid-December when the well was down to 1,100 feet, but without any new claims for oil and gas. The news from the nearby Whitlock well overshadowed everything else at this time, and the Bear Springs drill hole probably shut down.[18]

C.H. Bouton, the Pinal Oil Co.'s first president, took over as drilling supervisor on August 1, 1928 and made rapid progress through hard shale and conglomerate to a depth of 1515 feet. Mr. Bouton at this time attempted a cement water shutoff at about 1450 ft. in expectation that the hole would soon strike an oil sand. The shutoff may have been effected, but by March 1929 the hole was no deeper. It eventually reached 1552 feet. The new officers ceased drilling and the well evidently remained shut down after 1928. There were reports of activity as late as June 1931, but the new people listed as a field manager and fiscal agent suggests that the business was in receivership. The well itself never produced more than the reported early showings of oil and gas. The later homestead case file on this location claimed that the land had a water well and that the Pinal No. 1 oil well was 1551 ft. deep with water in it, flowing about five gallons a minute. As of 1938, the U.S. Geological Survey reported that this well discharged a "2-inch pipe full" of lukewarm water.[19] There is no flow at present.

Other wells, as many as eight or nine, were being drilled in what were then called the Willcox, San Simon, and Bowie fields. Some would shut down and new operations would begin, so that several wells were usually being drilled at any one time. The onset of the Depression in late 1929 probably had less effect on drilling activity than did the continuing failure to bring in a producing oil well. All of these were what we now call dry holes, though some continue in use today as water wells.

Throughout the "boom" the name of Bob Thomas, business agent for the Bear Springs Oil & Gas Co., kept coming up. He issued the news releases and may have been the person most responsible for keeping alive the hope that oil lay somewhere beneath the desert landscape in southeastern Arizona. He eventually filed a homestead entry at the Bear Springs Pinal 1 site, but he died on November 2 of that same year (1932).

In the face of the $80,000 to $100,000 reportedly expended on some wells, with no return, the small Arizona-based oil companies soon disappeared. Neither doodle-bugs nor modern geoscience has led to a discovery of oil beneath the sands of the San Simon Valley.

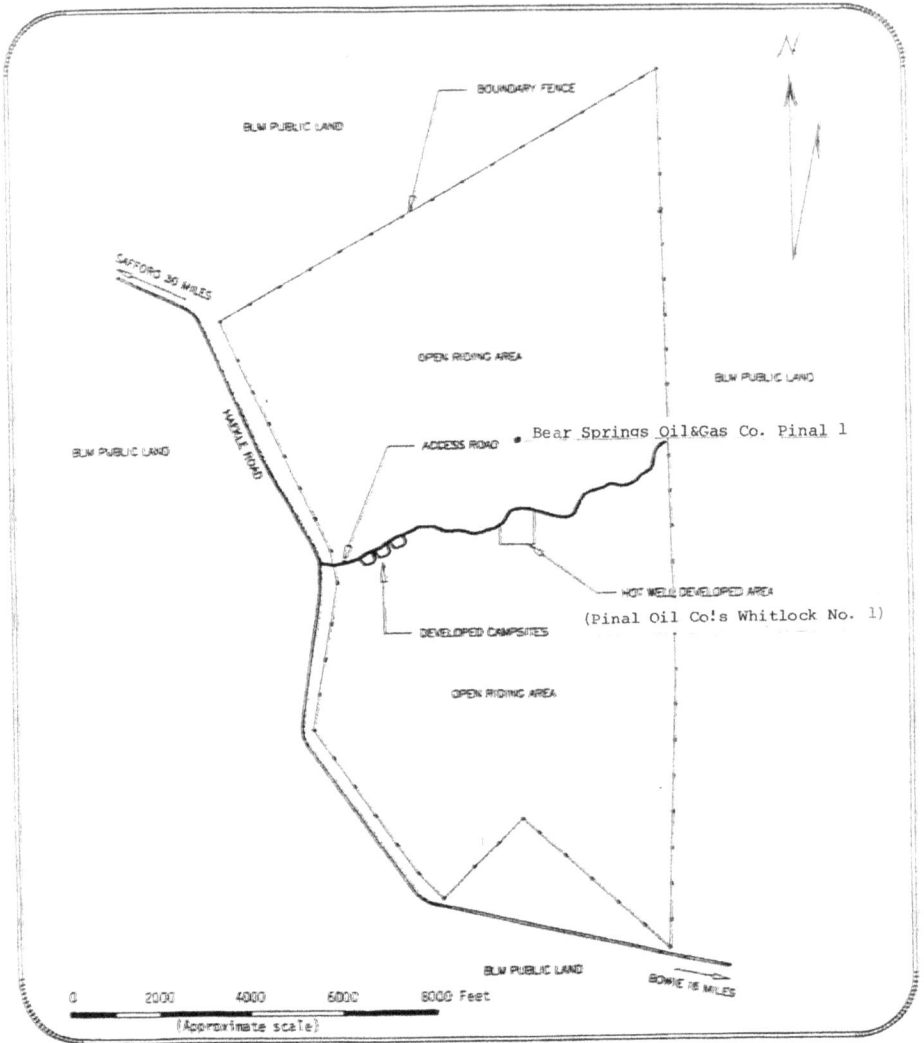

Map of Hot Well Dunes Recreation Area.
(Map courtesy of the U.S. Bureau of Land Management, Safford District)

A Flow of Warm Water from Pinal Oil Co.'s Whitlock No. 1 Well (post-1927 Photograph).
(U.S. Geological Survey Water-Supply Paper 796-F (1938))

Seven-foot diameter bull wheel and spool assembly, including spooling flanges, from Pinal Oil Co.'s Whitlock No. 1 oil drilling rig. (Photograph courtesy of the author, July 1996)

A-frame assembly of channel iron with eccentric arm, chain sprocket, and belt drums, from Pinal Oil Co.'s Whitlock No. 1 oil drilling rig. (Photograph courtesy of the author, July 1996)

NOTES

1. "Mine Tales: Though not exactly Texas, Arizona does have oil" (http://tucson.com/news/local/mine-tales-though-not exactly-texas); "Arizona Oil and Gas Conservation Commission" (http://www.azogcc.az.gov/content/what-are-recent-production); "Arizona Field Production of Crude Oil" (http://wwwhttp://.www.eia/.gov/dnav/pet/hist/Leaf-Handler).
2. *The Bulletin* (Solomonville, Az.), January 1, 1897.
3. Arizona Bureau of Mines (Arizona Geological Survey), *Mineral and Energy Resources of Arizona*, p. 71. Bulletin 180, The University of Arizona, 1969.
4. Stipp, Thomas F., and Helen M. Belkman, *Map of Arizona Showing Oil, Gas, and Exploratory Wells, Pipelines, and Areas of Igneous and Metamorphic Rocks.* Oil and Gas Investigations Map OM-201. Washington, U.S. Geological Survey, 1959.
5. *Graham County Guardian and Gila Valley Farmer* (hereafter GCG), August 5, 1927, p. 10.
6. "Searching for Oil in Arizona," *The San Simon Valley Oil News*, March 22, 1929, p. 1. The listed depth of this well is only 900 feet.
7. GCG, November 4, 1927, p. 1.
8. GCG, August 5, 1927, p. 10; Arizona Bureau of Mines (1969), p. 70.
9. "New Company Enters Oil District North of Bowie, in Arizona," clipping from a Holbrook, Az. newspaper, March 18, 1927; "Arizona May Assume Place As An Oil-Producing Area; Bowie Field Draws Interest," *The Arizona Republican*, April 8, 1927; *The Arizona Republican,* December 4, 1927; GCG, May 13, 1927, p. 5; July 15, 1927, p. 8; November 25, 1927, p. 8; "The Pinal Oil Co. and Its President,," *The San Simon Valley Oil News*, November 2, 1928.
10. GCG, February 17, 1928, p. 6,
11. "Monthly Oil Review of Southeastern Arizona," *San Simon Valley Tribune*, June 19, 1931, p. 1.
12. *The Arizona Republican*, December 4, 1927 (photo).
13. GCG, August 26, 1927, p.2; November 25, 1927, p. 1; *The Arizona Republican*, December 4, 1927; "Water-Shut-Off to be Made in Well, is Northeast of Bowie," *Arizona Record* (Globe, Az.), December 4, 1927, p. 1; "Estimated Flow Out of 'Discovery Well' 1000-1500 Bls. Daily," unnamed

Tucson newspaper, December 5, 1927, p. 2; all clippings in files of the Arizona Geological Survey, Tucson.

14. *The Arizona Republican*, December 4, 1927.

15. Articles of Incorporation and Annual Reports for the Bear Springs Oil and Gas Co., 1926-1931, on file with the Arizona Corporation Commission, Phoenix.

16. Articles of Incorporation and Annual Reports for the Pinal Oil Co., 1927–1930, on file with the Arizona Corporation Commission, Phoenix.

17. Clipping from a Holbrook, Az. newspaper, March 18, 1927, in files of the Arizona Geological Survey, Tucson. GCG, April 8, 1927, p. 3; May 6, 1927, p. 10. *The Arizona Republican*, December 4, 1927; extracts from the Canfield report, May 1, 1928, unpublished manuscript in files of the Arizona Geological Survey, Tucson.

18. GCG, September 30, 1927, p. 1; October 7, 1927, p. 10, December 16, 1927, p. 13; *The San Simon Valley Oil News*, December 16, 1927, p. 13; November 2, 1928, p. 1.

19. *The San Simon Valley Oil News*, November 2, 1928, p. 1; March 22, 1929, p. 1; GCG June 5, 1931, p. 9; June 19, 1931, p. 2; *San Simon Valley Tribune*, June 19, 1931, p. 1; *Tombstone Epitaph*, September 3, 1931; National Archives, Pacific Southwest Region, Record Group 49 (Bureau of Land Management), cancelled homestead entry PHX-071867; Maxwell M. Knechtel, *Geology and Ground-Water Resources of the Valley of Gila River and San Simon Creek, Graham County, Arizona* (U.S. Geological Survey Water-Supply Paper 796-F, p. 214. Washington: Government Printing Office, 1938.

An earlier version of this chapter appeared in the February 1997 issue of *Arizona Senior World*.

Suggested Reading

Altshuler, Constance Wynn, editor. *Latest from Arizona! The Hesperian Letters, 1859–1861.* Tucson: Arizona Pioneers Historical Society, 1969.

Barnes, Will C. *Arizona Place Names.* Tucson: University of Arizona Press, 1988.

Brooks, James F. *Mesa of Sorrows: A History of the Awat'ovi Massacre.* New York: W.W. Norton & Company, 2015.

Browne, J. Ross. *Adventures in the Apache Country* (a reprint of his *A Tour Through Arizona and Sonora*, 1864). Tucson: University of Arizona Press, 1974.

Canty J. Michael, and Michael N. Greeley, editors. *History of Mining in Arizona, Volumes I and II.* Tucson: Mining Club of the Southwest and American Institute of Mining Engineers Tucson Section, 1987 and 1991.

Finch, L. Boyd. *Confederate Pathway to the Pacific: Major Sherod Hunter and Arizona Territory, C.S.A.* Tucson: The Arizona Historical Society, 1996.

Fontana, Bernard L. *Calabazas of the Río Rico.* Tucson: Tucson Corral of the Westerners, Smoke Signal No. 24, 1971.

"Images of America" series, including *Buckeye, Globe, Early Yuma, The Phoenix Area's Parks and Preserves* and other titles. Arcadia Publishing, Inc., 2006–2009.

Johnson, Michael G. *American Indian Tribes of the Southwest.* New York: Osprey Publishing, 2013.

Kessell, John L. *Friars, Soldiers, and Reformers: Hispanic Arizona and the Sonora Mission Frontier 1767–1856.* Tucson: The University of Arizona Press, 1976.

McCarty, Kieran. *Desert Documentary: The Spanish Years, 1767–1821.* Tucson: Arizona Historical Society Historical Monograph No. 4, 1976.

Myers, John M. *Tombstone's Early Years.* Lincoln: University of Nebraska Press, 1995.

Myrick, David F. *Railroads of Arizona Vol. I, The Roads of Southern Arizona.* San Diego: Howell-North Books, 1981.

Summerhayes, Martha. *Vanished Arizona*: Lincoln: University of Nebraska Press, 1979, and other reprint editions.

Sweeney, Edwin R. *Cochise, Chiricahua Apache Chief.* Norman: University of Oklahoma Press, 1991.

Trimble, Marshall. *Arizoniana*: Phoenix: Golden West Publishers, 2004.

———, Marshall. *In Old Arizona.* Phoenix: Golden West Publishers, 2004.

———, Marshall. *Roadside History of Arizona.* Missoula: Mountain West Publishing Company, 1986.

Walker, Henry P. and Don Bufkin. *Historical Atlas of Arizona.* Norman: University of Oklahoma Press, 1979.

Williams, Jack. *San Augustín del Tucson,* and *The Presidio of Santa Cruz de Terrenate.* Tucson: Tucson Corral of the Westerners, Smoke Signal Nos. 47 & 48, 1986.

www.ingramcontent.com/pod-product-compliance
Lightning Source LLC
Chambersburg PA
CBHW031143090426
42738CB00008B/1197